EXERCISES IN HELPING SKILLS

A Training Manual to Accompany The Skilled Helper

THIRD EDITION

EXERCISES IN HELPING SKILLS

A Training Manual to Accompany The Skilled Helper

Gerard Egan

Loyola University of Chicago

Brooks/Cole Publishing Company
Monterey, California

Brooks/Cole Publishing Company
A Division of Wadsworth, Inc.

Printed in the United States of America

10 9 8 7 6 5 4

BF637.C6E38   1985   158'.3   85-14956

ISBN 0-534-05905-8

Sponsoring editor: Claire Verduin
Production editor: Barbara Kimmel
Cover design: Katherine Minerva

Contents

No

Part One

Introduction

The exercises in this manual are meant to accompany the revised edition of <u>The Skilled Helper</u> by Gerard Egan (Brooks/Cole Publishing Company, Monterey, California, 1986). These exercises serve a number of purposes:

(1) They can help you develop a <u>behavioral</u> rather than merely a cognitive grasp of the principles, skills, and methods that turn helping models into useful tools.

(2) They can be used by you to help you explore your own strengths and weaknesses as a helper. That is, they provide a way of having you apply the helping model to <u>yourself</u> first before trying it out on others. As such, they can help you confirm strengths that enable you to be with clients effectively and manage weaknesses that would stand in the way of helping clients manage problem situations.

(3) You can help clients use these exercises to explore and manage their own problems in living more effectively. These exercises provide one way of promoting client participation in the helping process.

(4) You can help clients use these exercises to learn the skills of problem management themselves. This kind of training-as-treatment can encourage self-responsibility in clients and help make them less dependent on others in managing their lives.

A TRAINING PROGRAM

The following are standard steps in a skills-training program:

(1) First, develop a <u>cognitive understanding</u> of a particular skill or counseling method. You can do this by reading the text and listening to lectures.

(2) <u>Clarify</u> what you have read or heard. This can be done through questioning and discussion.

The objective of Steps 1 and 2 is <u>cognitive clarity</u>.

(3) Watch experienced instructors <u>model</u> the skill or method in question. This can be done "live" or through films and videotapes.

(4) <u>Use</u> the skill or method you have read about and seen demonstrated. The instructor will provide the format for the initial use of skills and techniques. The purpose of this is to demonstrate to yourself that you understand the communication skill or helping method enough to begin to practice it.

The objective of Steps 3 and 4 is <u>behavioral clarity</u>.

(5) Move into smaller groups to <u>practice</u> the skill or method in question with your fellow trainees.

(6) During these practice sessions evaluate your own performance and get feedback from a trainer and from your fellow trainees. This feedback serves to confirm what you are doing right and to correct what you are doing wrong. The use of video to provide feedback is most helpful. (7) Finally, from time to time stop and reflect on the training process itself. Take the opportunity to express how you feel about the training process and how you feel about your own progress. While Steps 1 through 6 deal with the task of the training group, Step 7 deals with maintenance, that is, seeing to the feelings and needs of individual trainees. Effective processing helps establish a learning community.

The exercises in this manual can be used as a way of practicing the skills and methods "in private" before practicing them with your fellow trainees. They provide a behavioral link between the introduction to a skill or method that takes place in the first four steps of this training format and actual practice in a group.

THE STAGES AND STEPS OF THE HELPING PROCESS

For the most part the exercises presented here are grouped around and follow the order of the three stages and nine steps of the helping process. Here is an outline of the model.

STAGE I: Exploring The Present Scenario

Clients can neither manage problem situations nor develop unused opportunities unless they identify and understand them. Exploration and clarification of problems and opportunities take place in Stage I. This stage deals the current state of affairs, that is, the problem situations or unused opportunities which prompt clients to come for help. This stage includes the following steps:

1. Helping clients tell their stories. First of all, clients need to tell their stories. Some do so easily, others with a great deal of difficulty. You need to develop a set of attitudes and of communication skills that will enable you to help clients reveal problems in living and unused potential. This means helping clients find out what's going wrong and what's going right in their lives. Successful assessment helps clients identify both problems and resources.

2. Helping clients focus on significant concerns. This means helping clients identify the particular concern or concerns they want to deal with and explore and clarify these concerns. Effective counselors help clients work on high-leverage issues, that is, issues that will make a difference in clients' lives. They also help clients spell out problem situations in terms of specific experiences, behaviors, and feelings.

2

3. <u>Helping clients develop new perspectives</u>: This means helping clients manage <u>blind spots</u>, that is, helping them see themselves, their concerns, and the context of their concerns more objectively. This enables clients to see more clearly not only their problems and unused opportunities, but also in ways in which they want their lives to be different.

STAGE II: Developing a Preferred Scenario

Once clients understand either problem situations or opportunities for development more clearly, they may need help in determining what they would like to see different. They need to develop a preferred scenario, that is, a picture of a better future. For instance, a person out of work can be helped to picture the kinds of jobs he or she might like.

1. <u>Constructing a new scenario</u>. Since the current state of affairs is unacceptable, the client needs to be helped to create a vision of a new state of affairs. In marriage counseling, the new scenario might be, in generic terms, a better marriage. Some of the possible elements of this better marriage could be greater mutual respect, fewer fights, more effectively managed conflicts, the surrendering of grudges, the elimination of extramarital encounters, and so forth. The new scenarios or scenario elements constitute possible <u>goals</u> for the client.

2. <u>Evaluating the new scenarios</u>. Goals, if they are to translated into action, need to be clear, specific, realistic, adequately related to the problem situation, in keeping with the client's values, and capable of being accomplished within a reasonable time frame. Many clients need help in establishing goals or outcomes with these characteristics.

3. <u>Choosing goals and assuring commitment</u>. Some clients need help in making a final choice of goals and in committing themselves to them. While helpers are not responsible for their clients' sense of commitment, they can help them in their search for <u>incentives</u> for commitment.

STAGE III: Getting the Preferred Scenario on Line

Ultimately, clients must act in order to manage their problems in living and develop unused potential. The new scenario expressed in specific and realistic goals indicate <u>what</u> the client wants to achieve. But the client may need help in determining <u>how</u> he or she is to achieve these goals.

1. <u>Developing strategies for action</u>. You can help clients discover a variety of ways and means of accomplishing their goals. Often clients fail to use their imagination; they see only one way of accomplishing a goal.

2. <u>Formulating a plan</u>. Once clients are helped to choose strategies that <u>best fit</u> their style, resources, and environment, they need to

assemble these strategies into a <u>plan</u>. A plan indicates precisely what the client is to do and when.

3. <u>Action: The implementation of the plan</u>. Clients often need both support and challenge from helpers to implement plans. Counselors can also help clients monitor their progress.

The stages and steps of the helping model are illustrated graphically below. They are presented in a compact, linear way. But, as you shall soon learn from experience, helping is not as "neat," linear, and compact as the graphics suggest.

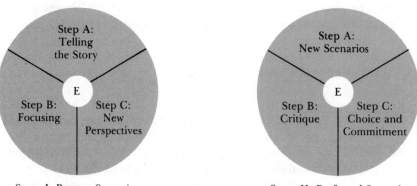

Stage I: Present Scenario

Stage II: Preferred Scenario

Stage III: Action—Getting
the New Scenario On Line

Figure 1: The Stages and Steps of the Helping Process

A NONLINEAR RELATIONSHIP APPROACH TO HELPING

Helping usually does not take place in the step-by-step linear fashion suggested by the stages and steps of the helping model. Effective helpers start wherever there is a client need. For instance, if a client needs support and challenge to commit himself or herself to realistic goals that have already been chosen, then the counselor tries to be helpful at this point. The nine steps of the helping model are ways of being with clients in their attempts to manage problems in living and develop unused potential. You can be with clients in both supportive and challenging ways as they attempt to:

* tell their stories.
* choose issues to work on that have payoff potential.
* deal with blind spots and develop new perspectives.
* develop a range of alternate scenarios.
* set realistic goals.
* commit themselves to these goals.
* develop strategies for accomplishing goals.
* formulate realistic action plans.
* implement plans.

The needs of your clients and not the logic of a helping model should determine your interactions with them.

YOUR ROLE AS TRAINEE: DEALING WITH REAL CONCERNS

One way of learning the stages and steps of this helping model is to apply them to your own problems and concerns first. This means placing yourself in the role of a client. There are two ways of doing this. You can pretend to be a client or you can really become a client. Since this distinction is important, let us look at it more carefully.
Role-playing versus dealing with real concerns. As a trainee, you are going to be asked to act both as a helper and as a client in practice sessions. In the written exercises in this manual, you are asked at one time or another to play each of these roles. There are two ways of playing the role of the client:

1. you can role-play, that is pretend to have certain problems, or
2. you can discuss your own real problems and concerns.

Role-playing, although not easy, is still less personally demanding than discussing your own real life concerns in practice sessions. Although some role-playing might be useful at the beginning of the training process (since it is less threatening and allows you to ease yourself into the role of client), I suggest that you eventually use the training process to look at some of the real problems or concerns in your own life, especially issues that might interfere with your effectiveness as a helper. For instance, if you tend to be an impatient person--one who places unreasonable demands on others--you will have to examine and change this behavior if you want to become an effective helper. Or if you are very nonassertive, this may keep you from helping clients make reasonable demands on themselves.

5

<u>Learning what it means to be a client</u>. Another reason for using real problems or concerns when you take the role of the client is that it gives you some experience of <u>being</u> a client. Then, when you face real clients, you can appreciate some of the misgivings they might have in talking to a relative stranger about the intimate details of their lives. Other things being equal, I would personally prefer going to a helper who has had some experience in being a client.

<u>The safe and productive training group</u>. Dealing with personal concerns in the training sessions will be both safe and productive if you have a competent trainer who provides adequate supervision for this process, if the training group becomes a learning community which provides both support and reasonable challenge for its members, and if you are willing to discuss personal concerns. Self-disclosure will be counterproductive if you let others extort it from you or if you attempt to extort it from others. Your self-disclosure should always remain appropriate to the goals of the training group. "Secret-dropping" and dramatic self-disclosure are counterproductive.

<u>Preparing for self-disclosure</u>. If you are to talk about yourself during the practice sessions, you should take some care in choosing what you are going to reveal about yourself. Making some preparation for what you are going to say can prevent you from revealing things about yourself that you would rather not. Here is a limited sample of the kinds of problems, issues, and concerns that trainees have dealt with during the training process.

* I'm shy. My shyness takes the form of being afraid to meet strangers and being afraid to reveal myself to others.
* I'm a fairly compliant person. Others can push me around and get away with it.
* I get angry fairly easily and let my anger spill out on others in irresponsible ways. I think my anger is often linked to my not getting my own way.
* I'm a lazy person. I find it especially difficult to expend the kind of energy necessary to listen to and get involved with others.
* I'm somewhat fearful of persons of the opposite sex. This is especially true if I think they are putting some kind of demand on me for closeness. I get nervous and try to get away.
* I'm a rather insensitive person, or so I have been told. I'm a kind of bull-in-the-china-shop type. Not much tact.
* I'm overly controlled. I don't let my emotions show very much. Sometimes I don't even want to know what I'm feeling myself.
* I like to control others, but I like to do so in subtle ways. I want to stay in charge of interpersonal relationships at all times.
* I have a strong need to be liked by others. I seldom do anything that might offend others or that others would not approve of. I have a very strong need to be accepted.
* I have few positive feelings about myself. I put myself down in a variety of ways. I get depressed a lot.
* I never stop to examine my values. I think I hold some conflicting values. I'm not even sure why I'm interested in becoming a helper.
* I feel almost compelled to help others. It's part of my religious background. It's as if I didn't even have a choice.
* I'm sensitive and easily hurt. I think I send out messages to others that say "be careful of me."

* I'm overly dependent on others. My self-image depends too much on what others think of me.
* A number of people see me as a "difficult" person. I'm highly individualistic. I'm ready to fight if anyone imposes on my freedom.
* I'm anxious a lot of the time. I'm not even sure why. My palms sweat a lot in interpersonal situations.
* I see myself as a rather colorless, uninteresting person. I'm bored with myself at times and I assume that others are bored with me.
* I'm somewhat irresponsible. I take too many risks, especially risks that involve others. I'm very impulsive. That's probably a nice way of saying that I lack self-control.
* I'm very stubborn. I have fairly strong opinions. I argue a lot and try to get others to see things my way. I argue about very little things.
* I don't examine myself or my behavior very much. I'm usually content with the way things are. I don't expect too much of myself or of others.
* I can be sneaky in my relationships with others. I seduce people in different ways--not necessarily sexual--by my "charm." I get them to do what I want.
* I like the good life. I'm pretty materialistic and I like my own comfort. I don't often go out of my way to meet the needs of others.
* I'm somewhat lonely. I don't think others like me, if they think about me at all. I spend time feeling sorry for myself.
* I'm awkward in social situations. I don't do the right thing at the right time. I don't know what others are feeling when I'm with them and I guess I seem callous.
* Others see me as "out of it" a great deal of the time. I guess I am fairly naive. Others seem to have deeper or more interesting experiences than I do. I think I've grown up too sheltered.
* I'm stingy with both money and time. I don't want to share what I have with others. I'm pretty selfish.
* I'm somewhat of a coward. I sometimes find it hard to stand up for my convictions even when I meet light opposition. It's easy to get me to retreat.
* I hate conflict. I'm more or less a peace-at-any-price person. I run when things get heated up.
* I don't like it when others tell me I'm doing something wrong. I usually feel attacked and I attack back.

This list is not exhaustive, but you can use it to stimulate your thinking about yourself and the kinds of dissatisfactions, problems, or concerns you may have about yourself, especially concerns that might relate to your effectiveness as a helper. The exercises in Step I-A will help you assess your satisfactions and dissatisfactions with yourself and your behavior. You can then choose the issues that you would like to explore during the training sessions.

SOME CAUTIONS

First, it is important to note that the exercises suggested in this manual are means, not ends in themselves. They are useful to the degree that they help you develop a working knowledge of the helping model and acquire the kinds of skills that will make you an effective helper.

Other exercises can be added and the ones outlined here can be modified in order to achieve this goal more effectively.

Second, these exercises have been written as an adjunct to the text. They often presuppose information in the text that is not repeated in the exercises.

Third, there may not be time to do all these exercises. Nor is it necessary to do all of them. What can be done depends on the length of the training program in which you are involved. However, a fairly wide sampling of these exercises can help you develop a behavioral feeling for the helping model and the kinds of skills involved in competent helping.

Fourth, these exercises achieve their full effect only if you share them with the members of your training group and receive feedback. Your instructor will set up the structure needed to do this. Since time limitations are always an issue, learning how to give brief, concise, behavioral feedback in a human way is most important.

Part Two

Basic Communication Skills

There are two sets of communication that are essential for helpers. The first set, included here in Part 2, includes attending, listening, basic empathy, and probing. The second set, dealing with the communication skills associated with challenging clients, is dealt with in Part 3 at Step I-C of the helping model. As the text notes, however, challenging can be part of any stage or step of the helping process.

EXERCISES IN ATTENDING

Your posture, gestures, facial expressions, and voice all send nonverbal messages to your clients. The purpose of the exercises in this section is to make you aware of the different kinds of nonverbal messages you can send to clients. It is important that what you say be reinforced rather than muddled or contradicted by your nonverbal messages.

Before doing these exercises, review the material on attending. Recall especially the basic elements of physical attending summarized by the acronym SOLER:

S   Face your clients SQUARELY. This says that you are available to work with them.

O   Adopt an OPEN posture. This says that you are open to your clients and nondefensive.

L   LEAN toward the client at times. This underscores your attentiveness and lets clients know that you are with them.

E   Maintain good EYE contact without staring. This tells your clients of your interest in them.

R   Remain relatively RELAXED with clients. This indicates your confidence in what you are doing and also helps clients relax.

Of course, these are guidelines rather than hard and fast rules. There are two points. First, use your posture, gestures, facial expressions, and voice to send messages you want to clients. Second, attend carefully so that you can listen carefully to clients.

EXERCISE 1:   Experiencing nonattending in the group conversation

1.   All the members of the training group (six to eight people) meet in a circle for a group discussion.
2.   A topic of conversation related to the training process is chosen (for instance, the fears of misgivings people have as they are about to enter training).
3.   All but one or two of the members maintain good attending posture. The other one or two violate the SOLER suggestions by slouching and so forth. However, they do participate verbally in the discussion.
4.   After about four or five minutes the conversation is stopped and the reactions of both attenders and nonattenders are discussed. For instance, how did you react to a member who was verbally present but nonverbally absent.

EXERCISE 2:   Attending as a demand for participation and intensity

1.   Each person in the training group finds a partner.
2.   They both assume a position of intense attending, including sitting close, facing each other squarely, maintaining good eye contact, and leaning forward.
3.   They then talk about the weather or some other trivial subject for about a minute or two.
4.   The conversation is stopped and they talk about whatever incongruity they felt between the attending position and the subject discussed.
5.   They discuss the proposition: Attending is itself a form of social influence; it places demands on clients for participation.

EXERCISE 3:   Observing and giving feedback on attending behavior

     In this exercise you are given an opportunity to observe the posture, gestures, facial expressions, and voice modulation of two people talking to each other.

1.   Divide into groups of four with members A, B, C, and D.
2.   A and B have a five-minute conversation in which they discuss what they like or don't like about their interpersonal styles. This conversation, as much as possible, should be a dialogue (that is, they should talk to and respond to each other and not just give speeches).
3.   Members C and D act as observers. They take written notes on A and B's attending behavior.
4.   After about five minutes, the conversation is stopped and C and D give A and B feedback, using the SOLER suggestions as a basis for the feedback. A caution: The purpose of this exercise is to give you an opportunity to observe attending and behavior and the nonverbal messages sent through such behavior. At this stage, it is best to note the variety of such behavior and how it affected you without interpreting it. While brief interpretations cannot be avoided

altogether, they should in no way become the focus of the feedback session. Your ability to interpret such behavior productively will grow with your experience. Describe what you see as important and mention briefly the impact it had on you.
5. After a four- or five-minute feedback session is completed, then the entire process is repeated with C and D as the speakers and A and B the observers.

Here are some typical feedback statements:

* "Most of the time you spoke very quickly, in spurts. I felt tense and nervous."
* "You sat very still throughout the conversation. Your hands remained folded in your lap, and there was practically no bodily movement."
* "When you talked about being a very sensitive person, one who is easily hurt, your voice became very soft and you stumbled over your words a bit. I wanted to be gentle with you."
* "You tapped your left foot almost constantly."
* "You put your hand to your mouth a great deal. It distracted me."
* "When your partner began talking about being shy, you leaned back and even moved your chair back a little. I felt you were giving her room to speak."
* "You broke eye contact a great deal when you were talking about yourself, but not when you were listening to your partner. It made me wonder what you were feeling when you talked about yourself."

Don't read too much into nonverbal behavior. In the training sessions make sure that your nonverbal behavior is helping you send the messages you want to send. Also observe the nonverbal behavior of your fellow trainees and give them feedback on how it affects you. Finally, ask others for feedback on your own nonverbal behavior.

EXERCISES IN LISTENING

There are four simple frameworks that help you listen to clients no matter whether they are just beginning to tell their stories or are at some other step of the model: (a) the content in terms of experiences, behaviors, and feelings and (b) the client's point of view.

Experiences, Behaviors, and Feelings

Clients talk, generally, about three things: their experiences, their behaviors, and the feelings associated with either or both. All of these can be overt, that is, external events capable of being seen by others, or covert, that is, inner events not capable of being seen by others.

<u>An experience</u>: something clients describe as <u>happening to</u> them:
    Overt: "He yelled at me."
    Covert: "Thoughts about death come out of nowhere and flood my mind."
<u>A behavior</u>: something clients <u>do or fail to do</u>.
    Overt: "I spend about three hours every night in some bar."
    Covert: "Before she comes over I plan everything I'm going to say."
<u>A feeling or emotion</u>: the <u>effect</u> associated with experiences or behaviors.
    Overt (expressed): "I got very angry and shouted at her."
    Covert (felt, but not expressed): "I was delighted that he failed, but I didn't let on."

You can learn a great deal about clients by listening to their manner of speaking, that is, the mix of experiences, behaviors, and feelings they discuss and how specific or vague they are. We start with emotions.

<u>EXERCISE 4: Listening to your own feelings and emotions</u>

    If you are to listen to the feelings and emotions of clients, you should first be familiar with your own emotional states. A number of emotional states are listed below. You are asked to describe what you feel when you feel these emotions. Describe what you feel as <u>concretely</u> as possible: How does your body react? What happens inside you? What do you feel like doing? Consider the following examples.

<u>Example 1</u>

<u>Accepted</u>: When I feel accepted,

    I feel warm inside.
    I feel safe.
    I feel free to be myself.
    I feel like sitting back and relaxing.
    I feel I can let my guard down.
    I feel like sharing myself.
    I feel some of my fears easing away.
    I feel at home.
    I feel at peace.
    I feel my loneliness drifting away.

Example 2

Scared: When I feel scared,

My mouth dries up.
My bowels become loose.
There are butterflies in my stomach.
I feel like running away.
I feel very uncomfortable.
I feel the need to talk to someone.
I turn in on myself.
I feel useless.
I'm unable to concentrate.
I feel very vulnerable.
I feel like whining or crying.

In order to keep this from becoming just an intellectual exercise, try to picture yourself in situations in which you have actually experienced these emotions. Then write down what you see in your imagination. You don't have to do all of these. Try the ones you have difficulty with. It's important to listen to yourself when you are experiencing difficult emotions.

1. accepted
2. affectionate
3. afraid
4. angry
5. anxious
6. attracted
7. bored
8. belonging, in community
9. competitive
10. confused
11. defensive
12. disappointed
13. free
14. frustrated
15. guilty
16. hopeful
17. hurt
18. inferior
19. intimate
20. jealous
21. joyful
22. lonely
23. loving
24. rejected
25. repulsed
26. respect
27. sad
28. satisfied
29. shy
30. suspicious
31. superior
32. trusting

Once you have described how you feel when you feel these emotions, you should have a wider repertory of words, phrases, and statements both to describe your own emotional states and to identify emotional states in others. Listening to your own emotions is a prelude to listening to the emotions of others.

Although the feelings and emotions of clients are extremely important, sometimes helpers concentrate too much, or rather too exclusively, on them. As we shall see later, feelings and emotions need to be understood, both by helpers and by clients, in the context of the experiences and behaviors that give rise to them. On the other hand, some clients hide their feelings, both from themselves and from others. In cases like these, helpers need to be sensitive to the cues that can point to hidden emotions on the part of the client.

EXERCISE 5: Listening to the feelings of clients

Now that you have considered feelings and emotions in your own life, you can review your ability to identify emotions that are expressed by others or implied in what they say. Read the following statements; then write down a number of adjectives or phrases describing how the speaker feels. Consider the following example.

Example

A twenty-seven year old man is talking to a minister about a visit with his mother the previous day. "I just don't know what got into me! She kept nagging me the way she always does, asking me why I don't visit her more often. As she went on, I got more and more angry. (He looks away from the counselor and looks toward the floor.) I finally began screaming at her. I told her to get off my case. (He puts his hands over his face.) I can't believe what I did! I called her a bitch. (Shaking his head.) I called her a bitch about ten times and then I left and slammed the door in her face."

How does this person feel? embarrassed, guilty, ashamed, distraught, amazed, extremely disappointed with himself, remorseful

Note carefully: This man is talking about his anger, but at the moment he is feeling and expressing the emotions listed above. Now try your hand at the following cases.

1. A woman, 40, married, no children: "These counseling sessions have really done me a great deal of good! I enjoy my work more. I actually look forward to meeting new people. My husband and I are talking more seriously and decently to each other. There's just so much more freedom in my life!"

How does this person feel? _____

_____

How intense is the emotion or emotions and how do you know? _____

_____

2. A woman, 53, about to get divorced: "My husband and I just decided to get a divorce. (Her voice is very soft, her speech is slow, halting.) I really don't look forward to the legal part of it—(pause)—to any part of it to tell the truth. I just don't know what to expect. (She sighs heavily.) I'm well into middle age. I don't think another marriage is possible. I just don't know what to expect."

How does this person feel? _____

_____

How intense is the emotion or emotions and how do you know? _____

_____

3. A man, 45, with a daughter, 14, who was just hit by a car: "I should never have allowed my daughter to go to the movies alone. (He keeps wringing his hands.) I don't know what my wife will say when she gets home from work. (He grimaces.) She says I'm careless—but being careless with the kids—that's something else! (He stands up and walks around.) I almost feel as if I had broken Karen's arm, not the guy in that car. (He sits down, stares at the floor, keeps tapping his fingers on the desk.) I don't know."

How does this person feel? _____

_____

How intense is the emotion or emotions and how do you know? _____

_____

4. A woman, 38, unmarried, talking about losing a friend: "My best friend has just turned her back on me. And I don't even know why! (said with great emphasis) From the way she acted, I think she has the idea that I've been talking behind her back. I simply have not! (said with great emphasis) Damn! This neighborhood is full of spiteful gossips. She should know that. If she's been listening to those foulmouths who just want to stir up trouble. . . . She could at least tell me what's going on."

How does this person feel? _____

_____

How intense is the emotion or emotions and how do you know? _____

_____

5. A senior in high school, 17, talking to his girl friend: "My teacher told me today that I've done better work that she ever expected. I always thought I could be good at studies if I applied myself. (He smiles.) So I tried this semester and it's paid off."

How does this person feel? _____

_____

How intense is the emotion or emotions and how do you know? _____

_____

6. A trainee, 29, speaking to the members of his training group: "I don't know what to expect in this group. (He speaks hesitatingly.) I've never been in this kind of group before. From what I've seen so far, I,

well, I get the feeling that you're pros, and I keep watching myself to see if I'm doing things right. (Sighs heavily.) I'm comparing myself to what everyone else is doing. I want to get good at this stuff . . . (pause) . . . but frankly I'm not sure I can make it."

How does this person feel? _____

_____

How intense is the emotion or emotions and how do you know? _____

_____

7. A young woman, 19, speaking to a college counselor toward the end of her second year: "I've been in college almost two years now, and nothing much has happened. (She speaks listlessly.) The teachers here are only so-so. I thought they'd be a lot better. At least that's what I heard. And I can't say much for the social life here. Things go on the same from day to day, from week to week."

How does this person feel? _____

_____

How intense is the emotion or emotions and how do you know? _____

_____

8. A man, 64, who has been told that he has terminal cancer, speaking to a medical resident: "Why me? Why me? I'm not even that old! And I don't smoke or anything like that. (He begins to cry.) Look at me. I thought I had some guts. I'm just a slobbering mess. Oh God, why terminal? What are these next months going to be like? (Pause, he stops crying.) What would you care! I'm just a failure to you guys."

How does this person feel? _____

_____

How intense is the emotion or emotions and how do you know? _____

_____

9. A woman, 42, married, with three children in their early teens speaking to a church counselor: "Why does my husband keep blaming me for his trouble with the kids? I'm always in the middle. He complains to me about them. They complain to me about him. (She looks the counselor straight in the eye and talks very deliberately.) I could walk out on the whole thing right now. Who the hell do they think they are?"

What does this person feel? _____

_____

How intense is the emotion or emotions and how do you know? _____

_____

10. A bachelor, 39, speaking to the members of a life-style group to which he has belonged for about a year: "I've finally met a woman who is very genuine and who lets me be myself. I can care deeply about her without making a child out of her. (He is speaking in a soft, steady voice.) And she cares about me without mothering me. I never thought it would happen. (He raises his voice a bit.) Is it actually happening to me? Is it actually happening?"

How does this person feel? _____

_____

How intense is the emotion or emotions and how do you know? _____

_____

11. A girl in her late teens who is serving a two-year term in a reformatory speaking to a probation counselor: (She sits silently for a while and doesn't answer any question the counselor puts to her. Then she shakes her head and looks around the room)."I don't know what I'm doing here. You're the third counselor they've sent me to--or is it the fourth? It's a waste of time! Why do they keep making me come here? (She looks straight at the counselor.) Let's fold the show right now. Come on, get smart."

How does this person feel? _____

_____

How intense is the emotion or emotions and how do you know? _____

_____

12. A man, 54, talking to a counselor about a situation at work: "I don't know where to turn. They're asking me to do things at work that I just don't think are right. If I don't do them, well, I'll probably be let go. And I don't know where I'm going to get another job at my age in this economy. But if I do what they want me to, I think I could get into trouble, I mean legal trouble. I'd be the fall guy. My head's spinning. I've never had to face anything like this before. Where do I turn?"

How does this person feel? _____

_____

How intense is the emotion or emotions and how do you know? _____

_____

EXERCISE 6: Listening to experiences and behaviors

In this exercise you are asked to identify not only feelings and emotions but also the key or relevant experiences and behaviors that give rise to them. What experiences and what behaviors contribute to the way the client is feeling? In some cases the client's experience might be the key, in some cases his or her behavior, and in some cases both. Consider the following example.

Example

A seventh-grade boy talking to a teacher he trusts (all this is said in a halting voice and he does not look at the teacher): "Something happened yesterday that's bothering me a lot. I was looking out the window after school. It was late. I saw two of the guys, the bullies, beating up on one of my best friends. I was afraid to go down. . . A coward. . . . I didn't tell anyone, I didn't do anything."

Feelings: ashamed, guilty, down, miserable _____

Relevant experience: watching a good friend get beat up _____

Relevant behavior: failing to help his friend _____

In this case the client's behavior, not helping, seems to be key to how he is feeling as he talks with the teacher.

1. A young woman talking to a counselor in a center for battered women: "This is the third time he's beaten me up. I didn't come before because I still can't believe it! We're married only a year. After we got married, he began ordering me around in ways he never did before we got married. He'd get furious if I questioned him. Then he began shoving me if I didn't do what he wanted fast or right. And I just let him do it! I just let him do it! (She breaks down and sobs.) And now three beatings in about four weeks. Oh God, what's happened?"

Feelings: _____

Relevant experience: _____

Relevant behavior: _____

2. A girl, 12, talking to a psychologist at a time when her parents are involved in a divorce case: "I still want to do something to help, but I can't. I just can't! They won't let me. When they would fight and get real mean and were screaming at each other, I'd run and try to get in between them. One or the other would push me away. They wouldn't pay any attention to me at all. They're still pushing me away. They don't care

how I think or feel or what happens to me! My mother tells me that kids should stay out of things like this."

Feelings: _____

Relevant experience: _____

Relevant behavior: _____

3. A man, 25, in a counselor training group talking to the trainer: "I've been sitting here watching you give Peggy feedback. You're doing it very well. But I'm also saying to myself, 'Why isn't he that helpful and that careful with me?' I want the same kind of feedback, but you don't say much to me at all. I'm as active as anyone else in the group. I volunteer to act as both counselor and client. I don't know why you pass me by."

Feelings: _____

Relevant experience: _____

Relevant behavior: _____

4. A woman, 35, with two children, one four, one six, whose husband has deserted them talking to a social worker: "He's not sending me any money. I don't even know where he is. They're asking me for the rent and telling me that I'll be out if I don't come up with it. I've been to two different agencies and filled out all sorts of forms, but I don't have any money or food stamps yet. I've been getting food from my mother, but she's really got next to nothing. What am I supposed to do? I'll work, but who's to take care of the kids. I asked all around and there's no day-care center anywhere near here."

Feelings: _____

Relevant experience: _____

Relevant behavior: _____

5. A man, 53, talking to a counselor a few months after the sudden death of his wife. His two children are married and living in distant towns: "I miss her so. The house seems so empty. I work alone on computer programs. There's no one I talk to at work. Now there's no one at home. I walk around the house thinking of how I was with her in each room. At night sometimes I sit in the dark thinking of nothing. We had few friends, so no one calls. And I haven't seen either of the kids since the funeral."

Feelings: _____

Relevant experience: _____

Relevant behavior: _____

6. A woman, 63, in a hospital dying of cancer, talking to a member of the pastoral counseling staff: "I can understand it from my children, but not from my husband. I know I'm dying. But he comes here with a brave smile every day, hiding what he feels. We never talk about my dying. I know he's trying to protect me, but it's so unreal. I don't tell him that his constant cheerfulness and his refusal to talk about my sickness are actually painful to me. (She shakes her head.) I'm being careful of him!"

Feelings: _____

Relevant experience: _____

Relevant behavior: _____

7. A freshman in college talking to a counselor toward the end of his first year: "One week I find myself studying hard, working on the school paper, going to a talk on foreign affairs. The next week I'm boozing it up, looking around for a hot sex partner, and playing cards all day with the boys. It's like being two different people who don't even know each other! I like being in college, away from home and all that. But when I'm here I don't know what I want."

Feelings: _____

Relevant experience: _____

Relevant behavior: _____

8. Man, 70, arrested for stealing funds from the company where he has worked for 25 years, talking to his lawyer: "To tell you the truth, it's probably a good thing I've been caught. I've been stealing on and off for the last five or six years. It's been a game. It soaked up my energies, my attention, distracted me from thinking about getting old. Now I'm saying to myself: 'You old fool, what're you running from?' I've been forcing myself to try to make sense out of my life. You're probably thinking: 'It's about time, old guy.' I'm thinking it's as good a time as any."

Feelings: _____

Relevant experience: _____

Relevant behavior: _____

9. Woman, 37, married, with an unwanted pregnancy; she has two children, one in the seventh and one in the eighth grade; she is talking to another woman, her closest friend: "Ellen, I just don't know what to do. I've talked to my pastor, but I knew what he was going to say. He wasn't much help at all. Oh, God, I don't want another child! Not now! A couple of people I know just assume I'll have an abortion. That's what they'd do. I won't have an abortion, I just won't. But I don't want to have to restructure my life. I've had my children!"

Feelings: _____

Relevant experience: _____

Relevant behavior: _____

10. A boy, 11, who has been sexually abused by an older male relative, talking to a counselor (he speaks in a jerky, agitated voice): "I liked him a lot. He was always nice to me. He took me to ball games. He gave me spending money. I mean he was not some kind of jerk. He was really kind. He was drunk when it happened. I trusted him. I wasn't even sure what was happening. I don't know what to think. Maybe I shouldn't have said anything. He looked so awful when I saw him yesterday. I <u>had</u> to say something, didn't I?"

Feelings: _____

Relevant experience: _____

Relevant behavior: _____

11. A minister who has been having an affair with one of his parishioners talking to another minister: "I've never known anyone like her before. It was as if it didn't make any difference that both of us were married. I've never experienced such strong emotion. I can tell myself exactly what I should do. But I don't do it. We avoid talking about where all this is going to lead. I know in the back of my mind that my family and career and all that are on the line, but I keep it pushed back. There's doom on the horizon, but the present is so damn full!"

Feelings: _____

Relevant experience: _____

Relevant behavior: _____

The Client's Point of View: Empathic Listening

Empathic listening is listening to and understanding the client's point of view. Even when you think the client's point of view needs to be challenged, it is essential to <u>hear</u> it.

EXERCISE 7: Listening to the client's point of view

The following instructions apply to both A and B below.

1. Read the paragraph. Try to picture the clients saying what they say. Listen carefully.

2. Go over the paragraph sentence by sentence. Identify experiences, behaviors, and feelings.
3. Summarize the client's point of view. Do not evaluate it or contaminate it with your own point of view.

A. The following client is a 40-year-old woman who has just lost her job. She is talking about the events before, during, and after her being fired.

"Yesterday I was talking with one of the punch-press operators when my boss storms in and begins raking me over the coals for a work stoppage I had nothing to do with. I stood there in shock. I was so angry that I wanted to yell back at him, but I kept my cool. But all day I couldn't get it out of my mind. No matter what I was doing, it haunted me. I finally got so angry that I burst into his office and told him just what I thought of him. I even let him have it for a few lousy things he's done in the past. He fired me on the spot. Last night I was pretty depressed. And all day today I've been trying to figure out where I can get a new job or maybe how I can get my old job back."

What is this person's point of view? _____

_____

_____

_____

_____

B. This client is a 37-year-old man who is talking to a counselor for the first time. He has been referred by a doctor who has found no physical basis for a variety of somatic complaints.

"My wife keeps putting me down. For instance, last week she got a job without even discussing it with me. She didn't even ask me how I'd feel. She doesn't share what's going on inside. She makes big decisions without letting me in on the process. I'm sure she sees me as weak and ineffectual. She's just like her mother. My mother-in-law never wanted me to marry her. She was too good for me. Now my wife does everything to prove that her mother is right. She would never admit it, of course, but that's the way she is. I wouldn't be surprised that her goal is to earn more money than I do. I see other guys getting divorces for a lot less than I have to put up with. But that would make both of them happy. I asked her to come with me to see you and she laughed at me, she actually _laughed_ at me."

What is this client's point of view? _____

_____

_____

* Compare your summaries with those of your fellow group members.
* On the assumption that these two clients affect you differently, discuss the differences in your reactions and the bases for these differences.

EXERCISE 8: Understanding one another's points of view

1. Divide into groups of three. The roles in each group are speaker, listener, and observer.
2. Take a few minutes to prepare a statement on an issue that you believe to be important. You may jot down a few notes, but the statement is to be spoken, not read. The statement should be able to be delivered in less than a minute.
3. After determining who is to go first, the speaker delivers his or her statement to the listener, while the observer watches.
4. The listener listens carefully and then summarizes the point of view for the speaker. The listener begins with the phrase: "This, I believe, is your point of view."
5. Both the speaker and the observer give feedback to the listener on his or her accuracy.
6. The process continues until each member of the group has played all three roles.

EXERCISES IN BASIC EMPATHY

Basic empathy is the communication to another person of your understanding of his or her experiences, behaviors, and feelings from his or her point of view. It is a skill you need throughout the helping model. Because it helps communicate to clients that you understand their points of view, it is very useful in establishing and developing relationships with clients. The starting point of the entire helping process and each of its steps is the client's point of view, even when it needs to be challenged.

The exercises in the previous section emphasized your ability to listen to and understand the client's point of view. The exercises in this section relate to your ability to communicate this understanding to the client.

The formula for basic empathy is:

"You feel . . ."--followed by the right category of emotion and the right intensity,

"because . . ."--followed by the experiences and/or behaviors that give rise to the feelings.

Here are a few examples:

* "You feel hurt because she left town without calling you."
* "You feel annoyed with yourself because you don't do anything about the way she treats you."
* "You feel guilty because he put his pride aside and asked you directly for help and you didn't even answer him."

It goes without saying that empathy, to be effective, must be accurate.

EXERCISE 9: Communicating understanding of a client's feelings

Feelings and emotions can be identified in a variety of ways:

* by single words:

    I feel good.
    I'm depressed.
    I feel abandoned.
    I'm delighted.
    I feel trapped.
    I'm angry.

* by different kinds of phrases:

    I'm sitting on top of the world.
    I feel down in the dumps.
    I feel left in the lurch.
    I feel tip top.
    My back's up against the wall.
    I'm really steaming.

* by what is implied in a behavioral statement   (what action I feel like taking):

    I feel like giving up. (implied emotion: despair)
    I feel like hugging you. (implied emotion: joy)
    I feel like smashing him in the face. (implied emotion: severe anger)
    Now that it's over, I feel like dancing in the streets. (implied
        emotions: relief and joy)

* by what is implied in experiences that are revealed:

    I feel I'm being dumped on. (implied feeling: anger)
    I feel I'm being stereotyped. (implied feeling: resentment)

I feel I'm at the top of her list. (implied feeling: joy)
I feel I'm going to catch my lunch. (implied feeling: apprehension)

Note here that the implication could be spelled out:

I feel angry because I'm being dumped on.
I resent the fact that I'm being stereotyped.
I feel great because I believe I'm at the top of her list.
I'm apprehensive because I think I'm going to catch my lunch.

A number of situations involving different kinds of feelings and emotions are listed below. Picture yourself talking to this person. Note the four ways used to communicate to the other and understanding of his or her emotions.

<u>Joy</u>: This person has just been given a job she really wanted.
    <u>Single word</u>. You're happy.
    <u>A phrase</u>. You're on cloud nine.
    <u>Behavioral statement</u>: You feel like going out and celebrating.
    <u>Experiential statement</u>: You feel you got what you deserve.

Now express the following feelings and emotions in two different ways.

1. This woman is about to go to her daughter's graduation from college. She never thought that her daughter would make it through. She ends by saying, "I can hardly wait to get there."

a. _____

_____

b. _____

_____

2. This woman has just had her purse stolen. She had just cashed her bi-weekly paycheck and the money was in the purse. She ends by saying, "I've got all my bills to pay. I don't know what I'm going to do."

a. _____

_____

b. _____

_____

3. This man is awaiting the results of medical tests. He has been losing weight for about two months and has been feeling tired and listless all the time. He ends by saying, "I . . . well, I just don't know where I stand. Nobody said anything to me during the tests."

a. _____

_____

b. _____

_____

4. A perspective employer has just found out that this man has a criminal record. He had hoped that he would get the job and prove himself before anyone found out. He ends by saying, "When the man who interviewed me called me and told me that he had learned about my prison record, well, I didn't know what to say."

a. _____

_____

b. _____

_____

5. This woman has just lost a custody case for her children. She never dreamed that the court would award the children to her husband whom she sees as selfish and spiteful. She ends by saying, "It's all over now."

a. _____

_____

b. _____

_____

6. This young man has just been abandoned by his wife. They have been married for about a year. He thought that things were going fairly well. He ends by putting his head between his knees and saying, "Now what do I do?"

a. _____

_____

b. _____

_____

7. This man's boss has just told him that the project must be finished by the end of the week or else he could be demoted or even lose his job. He knows that he has not been as effective at work as he might be. He ends by saying, "I'm really up against it now."

a. _____

_____

b. _____

_____

8. This woman has been suffering from migraine headaches for a long time. They seem to be getting worse. So far nothing has helped her to reduce their number or to manage them once they start. She ends by saying, "Nothing seems to work! Is this going to be my life?"

a. _____

_____

b. _____

_____

9. This woman has been told that there might be a cure for her child's life-threatening illness. She also realizes that the cure might not work. She ends by saying, "It's got to work! "

a. _____

_____

b. _____

10. This man is talking about having to work two jobs to support his family. It's fortunate that he has both jobs, but he has no time for himself. He ends by saying, "It's as if life is about nothing else but work."

a. _____

_____

b. _____

_____

11. This man has just found out that he is being laid off for the third time this year. The economy is in bad shape. There are very few prospects around.

a. _____

_____

b. _____

_____

EXERCISE 10: Communicating empathy--experiences, behaviors, feelings

In this exercise you are asked to do two things: (a) use the "you feel . . . because . . ." formula to communicate empathy to the client; (b) recast your response in your own words while still identifying both feelings and the experience and/or behavior that underlies the feelings. Consider the following example.

Example

Married woman, 31, talking to a counselor about her marriage: "I can't believe it! You know when Tom and I were here last week we made a contract that said that he would be home for supper every evening and on time. Well, he came home on time every day this past week. I never dreamed that he would live up to his part of the bargain so completely!"

Formula: "You feel great because he really stuck to his word."

Nonformula: "He fulfilled the contract beyond your expectations. Now that's a very pleasant surprise!"

In this nonformula response, identify the feeling component and the experience/behavior component.

Now imagine yourself listening intently to each of the people quoted below. First use the "You feel . . . because . . ." formula; then use your own words. Try to make the second response sound as natural (as much like yourself) as possible. After you use your own words, check to see if you have both a "you feel" part and a "because" part in your response.

1. Man, 40, talking about his invalid mother: "I know she's using her present illness to control me. How could a 'good' son refuse any of her requests at a time like this? (He pounds his fist on the arm of his chair.) But it's all part of a pattern. She's used one thing or another to control me all my life. If I let things go on like this, she'll make me feel responsible for her death!"

Formula: _____

_____

Your own words: _____

_____

2. Woman, 25, talking about her current boyfriend: "I can't quite figure him out. (She pauses, shakes her head slowly, and then speaks quite slowly.) I just can't figure out whether he really cares about me,

or if he's just trying to get me into bed. I've been burned before; I don't want to get burned again."

Formula: _____

_____

Your own words: _____

_____

3. Businessman, 38, talking to a close associate: "I really don't know what my boss wants. I don't know what he thinks of me. He tells me I'm doing fine even though I don't think that I'm doing anything special. Then he blows up over nothing at all. I keep asking myself if there's something wrong with me, I mean, that I don't see what's getting him to act the way he does. I'm beginning to wonder if this is the right job for me."

Formula: _____

_____

Your own words: _____

_____

4. Woman, 73, in the hospital with a broken hip: "When you get old, you have to expect things like this to happen. It could have been much worse. When I lie here, I keep thinking of the people in the world who are a lot worse off than I am. I'm not a complainer. Oh, I'm not saying that this is fun or that the people in this place give you the best service--who does these days?--but it's a good thing that these hospitals exist."

Formula: _____

_____

Your own words: _____

_____

5. Seventh-grade girl to teacher, outside class: "My classmates don't like me, and right now I don't like them! Why do they have to be so mean? They make fun of me--well, they make fun of my clothes. My family can't afford what some of those snots wear. Gee, they don't have to like me, but I wish they'd stop making fun of me."

Formula: _____

_____

Your own words: _____

_____

6. High school counselor, 41, talking to a colleague: "Sometimes I think I'm living a lie. I don't have any interest in high school kids anymore. So when they come into my office, I don't really do much to help them. Most of them and their problems bore me. But I've been here now for twelve years. I like living around here. I try half-heartedly to work up some interest, but I don't get far."

Formula: _____

_____

Your own words: _____

_____

7. Man, 35, who has not been feeling well talking to a friend of his who is a nurse: "I'm going into the hospital tomorrow for some tests. I think they suspect an ulcer. (He fidgets.) But nobody has told me exactly what kind of tests. I'm supposed to take these enemas and not eat anything after supper this evening. I've heard rumors about these kinds of tests, but I'm not really sure what they're like."

Formula: _____

_____

Your own words: _____

_____

8. Graduate student, 25, to advisor: "I have two term papers due tomorrow. I'm giving a report in class this afternoon. My husband is down with the flu. And now I find out that a special committee wants to 'talk' with me about my 'progress' in the program."

Formula: _____

_____

Your own words: _____

_____

9. Woman, 43, talking to a counselor in a rape crisis center: "It was all I could do to come here. A friend told me to call the police. And then I'd become one of those stories you read in the paper everyday! Or they'd be asking me all sorts of questions. Ugh! I just want to forget it. I don't want to keep reliving it over and over again."

Formula: _____

_____

Your own words: _____

_____

10. Female high school student, 17, talking to a male counselor about an unexpected pregnancy: "I, well, I don't think I can talk about it here. (Pause) You being a man and all that. (Pause) What happens between me and my boyfriend and me and my family—well, that's all very personal. I don't talk to strangers about personal things."

Formula: _____

_____

Your own words: _____

_____

EXERCISE 11: Empathy with clients facing dilemmas

Clients sometimes talk about conflicting values, experiences, behaviors, and emotions. Responding empathically means communicating an understanding of the conflict. Consider the following example.

Example

A woman, 32, talking to a counselor about a possible abortion: "I'm going back and forth, back and forth. I say to myself, 'Okay, I'll have the abortion,' then that seems to handle my reluctance to have another child and it means that Bill [her husband] will be relieved. I don't especially want another child, but he's totally opposed to it. So an abortion seems to be a way out. But the very next moment I begin thinking about the abortion itself or, even worse, how I'll feel about myself afterwards, and then I'm back at square one."

Identify the conflict or dilemma: An abortion might solve some problems, but it might also create some new ones.

Formula: "In one way, you feel relieved when you think about having the abortion, because this will solve some very practical problems for you and Bill, but almost at the same time you feel apprehensive because you're not at all sure what having an abortion means to you."

Nonformula: "You're caught in the middle. Having an abortion might well solve some serious problems, and that would be a relief. But you're asking yourself, 'What price am I going to pay?'"

1. Factory worker, 30: "Work is okay. I do make a good living, and both my family and I like the money. My wife and I are both from poor homes, and we're living much better than we did when we were growing up. But the work I do is the same thing day after day. I may not be the world's brightest person, but there's a lot more to me than I use on those machines."

The conflict: Work is good, but work is also bad.

Formula: _____

_____

_____

Your own words: _____

_____

_____

2. Mental hospital patient, 54, who has spent five years in the hospital; he is talking to the members of an ongoing therapy group; some of the members have been asking him what he's doing to get out: "To tell the truth, I like it here. So why are so many people here so damn eager to see me out. Is it a crime because I feel comfortable here? (Pause, then in a more conciliatory voice.) I know you're all interested in me. I see that you care. But do I have to please you by doing something I don't want to do?"

The conflict: _____

_____

Formula: _____

_____

_____

Your own words: _____

_____

_____

3. Juvenile probation officer to colleague: "These kids drive me up the wall. Sometimes I think I'm really stupid for doing this kind of work. They taunt me. They push me as far as they can. To some of them I'm just another 'pig.' But every time I think of quitting--and this gets me--I know I'd miss the work and even miss the kids one way or another. When I wake up in the morning, I know the day's going to be full and it's going to demand everything I've got."

The conflict: _____

_____

Formula: _____

_____

_____

Your own words: _____

_____

_____

4. High school teacher, 50, to the principal: "Cindy Smith really got to me today. She's been a thorn in my side all semester. Just a little bitch. Asking questions in her 'sweet' way, but everyone knows she's trying to make an ass of me. Little snot! So I let her have it—I let it all come out and pasted her up against the wall—verbally, that is. She was the fool this time. You know me; I just don't do that kind of thing. I lost control, I have no love for Cindy, but it was a pretty bad mistake."

The conflict: _____

_____

Formula: _____

_____

_____

Your own words: _____

_____

_____

5. Widowed mother, 47, talking about her son, 17: "He knows he can take advantage of me. If he stops talking to me or acts sullen for a couple of days, I go crazy. He gets everything he wants out of me, and I know it's my own fault. But I still love him very much. After all, he stays here with me. I do have a man in the house. He's going to be going to college locally, so he'll be around for a good while yet."

The conflict: _____

_____

Formula: _____

Your own words: _____

_____

_____

EXERCISE 12:   The practice of basic empathy in everyday life

     If the communication of accurate empathy is to become a part of your
natural communication style, you will have to practice it outside formal
training sessions. That is, it must become part of your everyday
communication style or it will tend to lack genuineness in helping
situations. Practicing empathy "out there" is a relatively simple
process.

1.   Empathy is not a normative response in everyday conversations. Find
     this out for yourself. Observe everyday conversations. Count how
     many times in any given conversation empathy is used as a response.

2.   Next try to observe how often you use empathy as part of your normal
     style. In the beginning, don't try to increase the number of times
     you use empathy in day-to-day conversations. Merely observe your
     usual behavior. What kind of response do you use fairly frequently?

3.   Begin to increase the number of times you use accurate empathy. Be
     as natural as possible. Do not overwhelm others with this response;
     rather try to incorporate it gradually into your style. You will
     probably discover that there are quite a few opportunities for using
     empathy without being phony. Keep some sort of record of how often
     you use empathy in any given conversation.

4.   Observe the impact your use of empathy has on others. Don't set out
     to use others for the purpose of experimentation, but, as you
     gradually increase your use of this communication skill naturally,
     try to see how it influences your conversations. What impact does it
     have on you? What impact does it have on others?

EXERCISES IN THE USE OF PROBES

Review the material on probes before doing the exercises in this section. A probe is a statement or a question that asks a client to discuss an issue more fully. There are ways of getting at important details that clients do not think of or are reluctant to talk about. Probes can be used at any point in the helping process to clarify issues, search for missing data, and expand perspectives. For instance, In Step B of Stage I probes are used to help clients spell our problem situations and unexploited opportunities in terms of specific experiences, behaviors, and feelings. An overuse of probes can lead to gathering a great deal of irrelevant information.

EXERCISE 13: Probing for clarity of experiences, behaviors, and feelings

In this exercise a brief problem situation will be presented. You are asked to identify the kind of information in terms of experiences, behaviors, and feelings needed to make the problem clear. If such information were to be brought up and explored spontaneously by the client, then, of course, probes would not be needed. Consider the following example.

Example

A woman, 24, complains that her husband is both psychologically and physically abusive to her. She wonders whether she should get a divorce. What are some of the things that could possibly relate to the clarification of this problem situation?

* What their marriage is like outside times of abuse.
* What good points their marriage has.
* Other defects in their marriage.
* The behavioral form the abuse takes, what he actually does.
* The precipitating factors.
* The pattern of abuse, if any.
* When and where it takes place (public? private?).
* With what frequency.
* How she reacts to the abuse both at the time it is happening and later.
* How she feels about it.
* How long it has been going on.
* How disruptive it is of their marriage.
* How he seems to feel about it.
* How he reacts later.
* Whether he sees it as a problem.

* Whether they discuss the abuse.
* What solutions, if any, have been tried.
* Whether he is willing to seek help.
* Whether he would be willing to come to counseling with her.

There are possible areas for exploration. Information should be sought only to the degree that is relevant to managing the problem situation.

In the next two cases make a list of some of the factors--that is, potentially relevant experiences, behaviors, and feelings--that might have to be explored if the problem situation is to be clarified.

1. Grace, 19, an unmarried first-year college student, comes to counseling because of an unexpected and unwanted pregnancy. She knows that the father could be either of two young men.

As in the example above, list some factors that need to be clarified if this young woman is to see the problem situation clearly enough to make informed decisions on handling it.

_____

_____

_____

_____

_____

_____

_____

_____

_____

_____

_____

_____

_____

_____

2. You are a counselor in a halfway house. You are dealing with Tom, 44, who has just been released from prison where he served two years for armed robbery. That was the only offense for which he has ever been convicted. The halfway house experience is designed to help him reintegrate himself into society. Living in the house is voluntary. The

immediate problem is that Tom came in drunk last night. Yesterday was supposed to be a job search day for him. Drinking is against the rules of the house.

List some of the things that need to be clarified if Tom is to see the immediate problem situation clearly enough to make some reasonable decisions.

_____

_____

_____

_____

_____

_____

_____

_____

_____

_____

_____

_____

Share with the members of your group the areas chosen for probing. Discuss the reasons given for the choices. Choices should be based on and related to the helping model.

EXERCISE 14: Combining empathy and probes

In this exercise you are asked first to reply to the client with basic empathy and then follow it with a probe. Ask yourself what kind of information or clarification in terms of concrete and specific experiences, behaviors, and/or affect would help the client see the problem situation more clearly. Consider the following examples.

Example 1

A law student, 25, is talking to a school counselor: "I learned yesterday that I've flunked out of school and that there's no recourse. I've seen everybody, but the door is shut tight. What a mess! I have no idea how I'll face my parents. They've paid for my college education and this year of law school. And now I'll have to tell them that it's all down the drain."

Empathy: The whole situation sounds pretty desperate both here and at home. And it sounds so final.

What is needed to make the problem more concrete and clear?   Whom did he actually see and precisely what kind of refusals did he get.

Probe: I'm not sure who you mean by 'everybody' and what doors were shut.

    The counselor wants to make sure that the client actually did think of all possibilities.

Example 2

When the topic of moving out of the hospital is brought up in a therapy group a 54-year-old patient in a mental hospital says: "To tell you the truth, I _like_ it here. So why is everyone here so eager to get me out. Who says that I can't like it here? Is that a crime?"

Empathy: You resent it when people pressure you into thinking of leaving.

What is needed to make the problem more concrete and clear?   It would help to find out what needs are being met in the hospital, what makes it so rewarding for him. Those rewards might exist outside.

Probe: What are the main things you like about being in the hospital?

    First respond with empathy and then try to think of a probe that might make a difference. Vary the kinds of probes you use. Remember that this exercise is not meant to encourage you to use probes automatically. When probes do help a client move forward, think of using empathy rather than further probes.

1. High school senior to school counselor: "My dad told me the other night that I looked relaxed. Well, I don't feel relaxed. There's a lull right now, because of semester break, but next semester I'm signed up for two math courses, and math really rips me up. But I need it for science since I want to go into pre-med."

Empathy: _____

_____

Fruitful area for probing _____

_____

Probe: _____

_____

2. Woman, 27, talking to counselor about a relationship that has just ended (she speaks in a rather matter-of-fact voice): "I came back from visiting my parents who live in Nevada and found a letter from Gary. He said that he still loves me but that I'm just not the person for him. In the letter he thanked me for all the good times we had together these last three years. He asked me not to try to contact him because this would only make it more difficult for both of us."

Empathy: _____

_____

Fruitful area for probing _____

_____

Probe: _____

_____

3. Married man, 25, talking to a counselor about trouble with his mother-in-law: "The way I see it she is really trying to destroy our marriage. She's so conniving. And she's very clever. It's hard to catch her in what she's doing. You know, it's rather subtle. Well, I've had it! If she's trying to destroy our marriage, she's getting pretty close to achieving her goal."

Empathy: _____

_____

Fruitful area for probing _____

_____

Probe: _____

_____

4. Woman, 31, talking to an older woman friend: "I just can't stand my job anymore! My boss is so unreasonable. He makes all sorts of silly

demands on me. The other women in the office are so stuffy, you can't even talk to them. The men are either very blah or after you all the time, you know, on the make. The pay is good, but I don't think it makes up for all the rest. It's been going on like this for almost two years."

Empathy: _____

_____

Fruitful area for probing _____

_____

Probe: _____

_____

5. Man, 45, who has lost his wife and home in a tornado: "This happened to a friend of mine in Kansas about ten years ago. He never recovered from it. His life just disintegrated and nobody could do anything about it. . . . It's like the end of the world."

Empathy: _____

_____

Fruitful area for probing _____

_____

Probe: _____

_____

6. Divorced woman, 44, talking to a counselor about her drinking; she has just told her "story": "Actually, it's a relief to tell someone. I don't have to give you any excuses or make the story sound right. I drink because I like to drink; I'm just crazy about the stuff, that's all. But I'm under no delusions that telling you is going to solve anything. When I get out of here, I know I'm going straight to a bar and drink. Some new bar, new faces, some place they don't know me."

Empathy: _____

_____

Fruitful area for probing _____

_____

Probe: _____

_____

7. Man, 57, talking to a counselor about a family problem: "My younger brother--he's 53--has always been a kind of bum. He's always poaching off the rest of the family. Last week my unmarried sister told me that she'd given him some money for a 'business deal.' Business deal, my foot! I'd like to get hold of him and kick his ass! Oh, he's not a vicious guy. Just weak. He's never been able to get a fix on life. But he's got the whole family in turmoil now, and we can't keep going through hell for him."

Empathy: _____

_____

Fruitful area for probing _____

_____

Probe: _____

_____

8. Woman, 49, talking to a counselor about her relationship with her husband: "To put it frankly, my husband isn't very interested in me sexually anymore. We've had sex maybe once or twice in the last two or three months. What makes it worse is that I still have very strong sexual feelings. It seems they're even stronger than they used to be. I keep thinking about this all the time. He doesn't seem very interested at all. I don't know if he's got someone on the side. I'm not handling it well."

Empathy: _____

_____

Fruitful area for probing _____

_____

Probe: _____

_____

9. Man, 49, talking to a rehabilitation counselor after an operation that has left him with one lung: "I'll never be as active as I used to be. But at least I'm beginning to see that life is still worth living. I have to take a long look at the possibilities, no matter how much they've narrowed. I can't explain it, but there's something good stirring in me."

Empathy: _____

_____

Fruitful area for probing _____

_____

Probe: _____

_____

10. Mark and Lisa, a married couple both 33, after years of attempting
to have children finally adopted a baby girl, Andrea. Their
relationship, which up to then seemed quite good, began to disintegrate.
They are both thinking about divorce now, but feel very guilty because of
the child. Both of them say, "If we only had never adopted Andrea."

Empathy: _____

_____

Fruitful area for probing _____

_____

Probe: _____

_____

Part Three

Stage I:
Identifying and Clarifying
Problem Situations

The exercises in this section all relate to the steps of Stage I. However, as indicated in the text, the tasks of these steps are interrelated and cumulative. This is reflected in the exercises.

STEP I-A: HELPING CLIENTS TELL THEIR STORIES

As indicated earlier, both the basic communication skills and the skills of challenging to be reviewed later serve the entire helping model. They belong to all stages and steps. We now begin to address the stages and steps of the model itself. Stage I deals with problem identification and clarification. Step A in this stage deals with helping clients tell their stories, that is, outline problem situations that bring them to the helper in the first place.

The exercises in this section are designed to help you tell your own story, that is, to help you identify the problematic issues of your own life that might stand in the way of helping others. Careful execution of at least some of the exercises in this section will give you a list of problems or concerns that are neither too superficial nor too intimate for the training group. These exercises also introduce you to wide-band filters that can help you listen more creatively to clients. Once you use these exercises to help yourself tell your own story, you can find that you can use some of them to help your clients do the same. Once you get a feeling for these exercises yourself, you will know which ones may help your clients.

EXERCISE 15: What is going wrong and what is going right in my life

Sometimes a very simple structure can help you and your clients identify the major dimensions of a problem situation. This exercise asks you to identify some of the things that are not going as well as you would like them to go in your life ("what's going wrong") and some of the things you believe you are handling well ("what's going right"). It is important right from the beginning to help clients become aware of their resources and successes as well as their problems and failures. Problems can be handled more easily if they are seen in the wider context of successes and resources.

In this exercise, merely jot down in whatever way they come to you things that are going right and things that could be going better for you. In order to stress the positive, see if you can write down at least two things that are going right for everything you see going wrong. Read the list in the example on the next page and then do your own. Don't worry whether the problems or concerns you list are really important. Jot down whatever comes to your mind. Your own list may include some items similar to those in the example, but it may be quite different because it will reflect you and not someone else.

Example

What Is Going Right

I have a lot of friends.

I have a decent job and people like the work I do.

Others can count on me; I'm dependable.

I have a reasonable amount of intelligence.

I have no major financial diffi- culties; I'm secure.

My wife and I get along fairly well.

I am very healthy.

My belief in God gives me a kind of center in life, a stability.

What Is Going Wrong

I seem to have a very negative attitude toward myself.

I get dependent on others much too easily.

My life seems boring too much of the time.

I am afraid to take risks.

What Is Going Right

_____

_____

_____

_____

_____

_____

_____

_____

_____

What Is Going Wrong

_____

_____

_____

_____

_____

_____

_____

_____

_____

EXERCISE 16:   Reviewing the developmental tasks of life and the social
      settings in which they take place

In your efforts to manage your own life more effectively and to
help others do the same, it is useful to have a comprehensive model of
human functioning to help you listen to your own experience and that of
others in a focused way. Exercises 2, 3, 4, and 5 are based on the
People in Systems model developed by Egan and Cowan (Monterey, Calif.:
Brooks/Cole, 1979) and are designed to help you listen to your own
experience in a focused way in terms of (1) the developmental tasks you
face at your current stage of life, (2) the social settings in which you
live out your life, and (3) the life skills you need to carry out these
developmental tasks and involve yourself in growthful ways in these
social settings.

This exercise is a kind of checklist that can be used to take a
comprehensive "radar scan" of important areas of your life with a view to
identifying both resources and concerns. The purpose of the people-in-
systems model is to help you see your own, and eventually your clients',
concerns in as wide a context as possible.

In Exercise 2 you are asked to consider your experience with
respect to ten major developmental tasks of adult life and the social
settings in which these tasks are carried out. Again, it is most
important that you identify strengths as well as "soft" spots in these
developmental areas. Use extra paper as needed.

1. Competence: What Do I Do Well? Do I see myself as a person who is
capable of getting things done? Do I have the resources needed to
accomplish goals I set for myself? In what areas of life do I excel? In
what areas of life would I want to be more competent than I am?

           Strengths   Weaknesses

_____   _____

_____   _____

_____   _____

2. Autonomy: Can I Make It On My Own?   Can I get things done on my
own? Do I avoid being overly dependent or independent? Am I reasonably
interdependent in my work and social life? When I need help, do I find
it easy to ask for it? In what social settings do I find myself most
dependent? counterdependent? independent? interdependent?

           Strengths   Weaknesses

_____   _____

_____   _____

_____   _____

_____   _____

3. <u>Values: What Do I Believe In</u>?   What are my principal values? Do I allow for reasonable changes in my value system? Do I put my values into practice? Do any of my values I hold conflict with others? In what social settings do I pursue the values that are most important to me?

<u>Strengths</u>   <u>Weaknesses</u>

_____   _____

_____   _____

_____   _____

4. <u>Identity: Who Am I In This World</u>?   Do I have a good sense of who I am and the direction I'm going in life? Do the ways that others see me fit with the ways in which I see myself? Do I have some kind of center that gives meaning to my life? In what social settings do I have my best feelings for who I am? In what social settings do I lose my identity? In what ways am I confused or dissatisfied with who I am?

<u>Strengths</u>   <u>Weaknesses</u>

_____   _____

_____   _____

_____   _____

5. <u>Intimacy: What Are My Closer Relationships Like</u>?   What kinds of closeness do I have with others? Do I have acquaintances, friends, and intimates? What is my life in my peer group like? Are there other social groups in my life? What is it that I like in them?

<u>Strengths</u>   <u>Weaknesses</u>

_____   _____

_____   _____

_____   _____

6. <u>Sexuality: Who Am I As a Sexual Person</u>?   To what degree am I satisfied with my sexual identity, my sexual preferences, and my sexual behavior? How do I handle my sexual needs and wants? What social settings influence the ways I act sexually?

<u>Strengths</u>   <u>Weaknesses</u>

_____   _____

_____   _____

_____   _____

7. <u>Love, Marriage, Family</u>: <u>What Are My Deeper Commitments in Inter-personal Living?</u> What is my marriage like? How do I relate to family and relatives? How do I feel about the quality of my family life? If not married, in what ways do I look forward to marriage? What misgivings do I have?

Strengths   Weaknesses

_____   _____

_____   _____

_____   _____

_____   _____

8. <u>Career</u>: <u>What Is the Place of Work In My Life?</u> How do I feel about the way I am preparing myself for a career or the career I am currently pursuing? What do I get out of work? What is my workplace like? How does it affect me? What impact do I have there?

Strengths   Weaknesses

_____   _____

_____   _____

_____   _____

_____   _____

9. <u>Investment in the Wider Community</u>: <u>How Big Is My World?</u> How do I invest myself in the world outside of friends, work, and the family? What is my neighborhood like? Do I have community, civic, political, social involvements or concerns? In what ways am I optimistic about the world? In what ways am I cynical?

Strengths   Weaknesses

_____   _____

_____   _____

_____   _____

_____   _____

10. <u>Leisure</u>: <u>What Do I Do With My Free Time?</u> Do I feel that I have sufficient free time? How do I use my leisure? What do I get out of it? In what social settings do I spend my free time?

Strengths   Weaknesses

_____   _____

_____   _____

_____   _____

_____   _____

In your opinion, which strengths that you have noted will help you be a more effective counselor? In what specific ways?

_____

_____

_____

_____

_____

_____

_____

_____

_____

In your opinion, which weaknesses or problems you have noted might stand in the way of your being an effective helper? In what specific ways?

_____

_____

_____

_____

_____

_____

_____

_____

_____

_____

_____

EXERCISE 17: Conflicts in the network of the social settings of life

(1) Charting the social settings of life. Since you are a member
of a number of different social settings and since each places certain
demands on you, conflicts can arise between two or more settings. In
this exercise you are asked to write your name in the middle of a sheet of
paper. Then, as in the example (see page 152), draw spokes out to the
various social settings of your life. The person in the example is
Mitch, 45, a principal of an inner-city high school in a large city. He
is married and has two teenage sons. Neither attends the high school of
which he is principal. He is seeing a counselor because of exhaustion
and bouts of hostility and depression. He has had a complete physical
check-up and there is no evidence of any medical problem.

(2) Reviewing expectations, demands, concerns. Now take each
social setting and write down the expectations people have of you in that
setting, the demands they place on you, the concerns you have, the
dissatisfactions expressed to you. For instance, some of the things Mitch
writes are:

Faculty

* Some faculty members want a personal relationship with me and I have
neither the time nor the desire.
* Some faculty members have retired on the job. I don't know what to do
with them.
* Some of the white faculty members are suspicious of me and distant
just because I'm black.
* One faculty member wrote the district superintendent and said that I
was undermining her reputation with other faculty members. This is not
true.

Family

* My wife says that I'm letting school consume me; she complains
constantly because I don't spend enough time at home.
* My kids seem to withdraw from me because I'm a double authority
figure, a father and a principal.

Parents

* My mother is infirm; my retired father calls me and tells me what a
hard time he's having getting used to retirement.
* My mother tells me not to be spending time with her when I have so
much to do and then she complains to my wife and my father when I don't
show up.

Mitch goes on to list demands, expectations, concerns, and frustrations
that relate to each of the settings he has listed on his chart.
On a separate sheet of paper, list the demands, expectations, and
concerns related to each of the social settings you have on your chart.
Do not try to solve any of the problems you see cropping up. If some
solution to a problem does suggest itself while you are doing this
exercise, jot it down and put it aside.

(3) <u>Identifying conflicts between systems</u>. Once you review the expectations, demands, and concerns associated with each setting, list the conflicts <u>between settings</u> that cause you concern.

Here are some of the conflicts Mitch identifies:
* My wife wants me to spend more time at home and yet she criticizes me for not spending more time with my parents.
* The students, both individually and through their organizations, keep asking me to be more liberal while their parents are asking me to tighten things up.
* My administrative staff thinks that I'm taking sides against them in a dispute with the athletic department.
* My friends say that I spend so much time at work involving myself in crisis management that I have no time left for them; they tell me I'm doing myself in.

Now list any conflicts you see arising among the various social settings of your life.

_____

_____

_____

_____

_____

_____

_____

_____

_____

_____

_____

_____

_____

_____

_____

_____

EXERCISE 18: Assessing the impact of the larger organizations and
              institutions of society on your life

(1) Here is a list of some of the larger organizations and institutions
that might, directly or indirectly, affect your life and with which you
may have some concerns.

* newspapers   * federal government and its agencies
* television   * state government and its agencies
* the economy   * local government and its agencies
* the institutional church   * the food industry
* the insurance industry   * the mental health system
* the health-care industry   * education
* big business   * unions
* law enforcement agencies   * the courts
* transportation   * the energy industry
* professional athletics   * welfare agencies
* international tensions/crises

(2) Indicate any concerns you might have because of the ways in which
any of these institutions are affecting you. Some examples:

* "I think that the sex and violence on TV are harming my children, and
yet they complain bitterly when I restrict what they can see. They say
that other children get to see whatever they want and are not corrupted
by it."
* "I'm getting old and I haven't been able to save any money. I am very
afraid that I'll get sick and that Medicare won't really take care of
me. I keep looking forward to an awful old age. I don't know whether I
should put the little money I have into health insurance for the
elderly. But I saw a TV program the other night in which they talked
about health insurance for the elderly as a racket."
* "I've got a degree in counseling and I can't get a job. The people in
the schools say that I need to be certified as a teacher and have a
school psychologist degree. The people in mental health centers say
they are hiring only social workers. Government cuts mean that service
people are being laid off. No one yet has tried to find out whether I'm
good at my profession or not. I feel I'm being done in by the politics
of the whole situation."

     List any concerns you have that are related to the larger
organizations and institutions that are affecting your life:

_____

_____

_____

_____

EXERCISE 19: Assessing life skills

Sometimes people develop problems or fail to manage them because they do not have the kinds of life skills needed to handle developmental tasks and to invest themselves effectively in the social systems of life. For instance, a young married couple finds that they don't have the communication skills needed to talk to each other reasonably about the problems they encounter during the first couple of years of marriage.

This exercise is a checklist designed to help you get in touch with both your resources and possible areas of deficit. Listed below are various groups of skills needed to undertake the tasks of everyday living. Rate yourself on each skill. The rating system is as follows:

5. I have a very high level of this skill.
4. I have a moderately high level of this skill.
3. From what I can judge, I am about average in this skill.
2. I have some moderate deficit in this skill.
1. I have a serious deficit in this skill.

You are also asked to rate how important each skill is in your eyes. Use the following scale.

5. For me this skill is very important.
4. For me this skill is of moderate importance.
3. For me this skill has average importance.
2. For me this skill is rather unimportant.
1. For me this skill is completely unimportant.

Area A: Body-related Skills

	Level	Importance
* Knowing how to put together nutritional meals.	_____	_____
* Knowing how to control weight.	_____	_____
* Knowing how to keep fit through exercise.	_____	_____
* Knowing how to maintain basic body hygiene.	_____	_____
* Basic grooming skills.	_____	_____
* Knowing what to do when everyday health problems such as colds and minor accidents occur.	_____	_____
* Skills related to sexual expression.	_____	_____
* Athletic skills.	_____	_____
* Aesthetic skills such as dancing.	_____	_____

Other body-related skills:

* _____   _____ _____

* _____   _____ _____

* _____   _____ _____

Area B: Learning and Learning-How-to-Learn Skills

* Knowing how to read well.   ____ ____
* Knowing how to write clearly.   ____ ____
* Knowing basic mathematics.   ____ ____
* Knowing how to learn and study efficiently.   ____ ____
* Knowing something about the use of computers.   ____ ____
* Knowing how to see current issues in historical   ____ ____
  perspective.
* Knowing something about basic statistics.   ____ ____
* Knowing how to use a library.   ____ ____
* Knowing how to find information I need.   ____ ____

Other learning and learning-how-to-learn skills.

* _____ ____ ____

* _____ ____ ____

* _____ ____ ____

Area C: Skills Related to Values   ____ ____

* Knowing how to clarify my own values.   ____ ____
* Knowing how to identify the values of others   ____ ____
  who have a significant relationship to me.
* Knowing how to identify the values being "pushed"   ____ ____
  by the social systems to which I belong.
* Knowing how to construct and reconstruct my own   ____ ____
  set of values.

Other value-related skills:

* _____ ____ ____

* _____ ____ ____

* _____ ____ ____

Area D: Self-Management Skills

* Knowing how to plan and set realistic goals.   ____ ____
* Problem-solving or problem-management skills.   ____ ____
* Decision-making skills.   ____ ____
* Knowing and being able to use basic principles of   ____ ____
  behavior such as the use of incentives.
* Knowing how to manage my emotions.   ____ ____
* Knowing how to delay gratification.   ____ ____
* Assertiveness: knowing how to get my needs met   ____ ____
  while respecting the legitimate needs of others.

Other self-management skills:

*   _____   ____   ____

*   _____   ____   ____

*   _____   ____   ____

Area E: Communication Skills

*   The ability to speak before a group. ____   ____
*   The ability to listen to others actively. ____   ____
*   The ability to understand others. ____   ____
*   The ability to communicate understanding to others (empathy). ____   ____
*   The ability to challenge others reasonably. ____   ____
*   The ability to provide useful information to others. ____   ____
*   The ability to explore with another person what is happening in my relationship to him or her. ____   ____

Other communication skills:

*   _____   ____   ____

*   _____   ____   ____

*   _____   ____   ____

Area F: Skills Related to Small Groups

*   Knowing how to be an effective active member of a small group. ____   ____
*   Knowing how to design and organize a group. ____   ____
*   Knowing how to lead a small group. ____   ____
*   Team-building skills. ____   ____

Other small-group skills:

*   _____   ____   ____

*   _____   ____   ____

*   _____   ____   ____

Area G: Organization Involvement and Development Skills

*   The ability to be a contributing member of larger organizations or institutions. ____   ____
*   Managerial skills. ____   ____
*   Consultation skills. ____   ____
*   Conflict management and negotiation skills. ____   ____
*   Organizational design skills. ____   ____
*   The ability to organize efforts to change organizations or institutions. ____   ____

*   Community (neighborhood) development skills.   _____   _____
*   The skills of political involvement.   _____   _____

Other organization-involvement skills:

*   _____   _____   _____

*   _____   _____   _____

*   _____   _____   _____

Identify any skills deficits that are associated with the problems or concerns you have discovered so far. Indicate the skill and what problem or concern it relates to.

_____

_____

_____

_____

_____

_____

_____

What kinds of skills do you think you need to become better at; not just to handle your own problems more effectively, but to be an effective counselor?

_____

_____

_____

_____

_____

_____

_____

EXERCISE 20:   A sentence-completion assessment of problems

Exercises 6 and 7 deal with sentence completions. Do them quickly. They may help you expand in more specific ways what you have learned about yourself in preceding exercises.

1. My biggest problem is

2. I'm quite concerned about

3. One of my other problems is

4. Something I do that gives me trouble is

5. Something I fail to do that gets me into trouble is

6. The social setting of life I find most troublesome is

7. The most frequent negative feelings in my life are

8. These negative feelings take place when

9. The person I have most trouble with is

10. What I find most troublesome in this relationship is

11. Life would be better if

12. I tend to do myself in when I

13. I don't cope very well with

14. What sets me most on edge is

15. I get anxious when

16. A value I fail to put into practice is

17. I'm afraid to

18. I wish I

19. I wish I didn't

20. What others dislike most about me is

21. What I don't seem to handle well is

22. I don't seem to have the skills I need in order to

23. A problem that keeps coming back is

24. If I could change just one thing in myself it would be

EXERCISE 21: A sentence-completion assessment of strengths

1. One thing I like about myself is

2. One thing others like about me is

3. One thing I do very well is

4. A recent problem I've handled very well is

5. When I'm at my best I

6. I'm glad that I

7. Those who know me are glad that I

8. A compliment that has been paid to me recently is

9. A value that I try hard to practice is

10. An example of my caring about others is

11. People can count on me to

12. They said I did a good job when I

13. Something I'm handling better this year than last is

14. One thing that I've overcome is

15. A good example of my ability to manage my life is

16. I'm best with people when

17. One goal I'm presently working toward is

18. A recent temptation that I managed to overcome was

19. I pleasantly surprised myself when I

20. I think that I have the guts to

21. If I had to say one good thing about myself I'd say that I

22. One way I successfully control my emotions is

23. One way in which I am very dependable is

24. One important thing I intend to do within two months is

STEP I-B: FOCUSING AND PROBLEM CLARIFICATION

This step deals with two tasks. First of all, once clients tell their stories, there is need to determine just which issue or concern is to be considered first. As indicated in the text, this is called focusing and deals with the choice of issues that have leverage. Second, once a problem is chosen for consideration, it needs to be explored concretely. The exercises in these steps deal with these two tasks.

FOCUSING
Choosing Issues That Will Make a Difference

Often enough the stories clients tell are quite complex. And so they may need your help in deciding which issues to work on first. If they have a number of concerns, then choosing those which, if managed, will make a difference in their lives is important. Once an issue is chosen for exploration, you can help the client clarify it. In Step I-A you used a number of assessment exercises to identify some of your own concerns. It is time to decide which issues you would like to deal with during the training process.

EXERCISE 22: Choosing issues and concerns to explore

(1) First of all, merely list some of the concerns or unexploited opportunities you have discovered in doing the assessment exercises.

_____

_____

_____

_____

_____

_____

_____

_____

_____

_____

_____

_____

_____

_____

_____

_____

_____

_____

_____

_____

_____

_____

   (2) Next, apply the criteria listed below to each item on your
list. These are the criteria you use with clients to help them focus on
an issue for exploration and clarification.

* Severity or urgency. Is this an issue that needs more or less
immediate attention because of the distress it causes you or others
and/or because of its frequency or uncontrollability?

* Importance. Is this an issue that's important to you, important
enough to discuss and act on?

* Timing. Is this a problem that, in your estimation, can be managed at
this time with the resources you have available? Is this a concern which
is ripe for managing?

* Complexity. Is this concern a manageable part of a larger or more
complex problem situation? Can it be divided into more manageable parts?

* Promise of success. If this issue is focused on, is there some
probability that it can be managed successfully. If not, is this the
right place to start?

* Spread effect. Is this the kind of problem which, if handled, might
lead to improvement in other areas of your life?

* Control. Is this a problem under your control? To manage it more
effectively do you have to act or do you have to influence others to act?

* Cost effectiveness. Is it worth trying to deal with this concern,
that is, do the benefits of handling it outweigh the costs in terms of
time and effort?

* Substance. Is this issue worthwhile discussing? Is it capable of being developed over a number of sessions? On the other hand, is it too serious to be discussed now and in this setting?

* Willingness. Is this a concern or problem that you are willing to discuss with the members of your training group? Might you be willing to discuss it when you become more comfortable with the members of the group?

(3) With these criteria in mind, review the concerns you have just listed and indicate five concerns or problem areas of some substance which you would be willing to explore when you take the role of client in your training group.

a. _____

_____

_____

b. _____

_____

_____

c. _____

_____

_____

d. _____

_____

_____

e. _____

_____

_____

EXERCISES IN HELPING CLIENTS CLARIFY PROBLEM SITUATIONS

The exercises in this section relate to the skills you need to interview clients and help them explore and clarify the problems, issues, and concerns they come with. These skills are in addition to the basic communication skills already discussed In Part Two.

Assessment models such as the people-in-systems model help you listen to and organize the content of the client's disclosures. However, since problem situations cannot usually be managed more effectively until they are clarified, it is also necessary for you to listen to how concretely the client is talking about his or her problems in living. A problem situation or some part of it is clear if it is spelled out in terms of specific experiences, specific behaviors, and specific feelings in specific situations. As indicated in the text, each of these may be overt or covert.

EXERCISE 23: Speaking concretely about experiences

In this exercise, you are asked to speak of some of your experiences--first vaguely, then concretely. Read the following examples.

Example 1

* Vague statement of experience: "I'm sometimes less efficient because of a physical condition."
* Concrete statement of the same experience: "I get migraine headaches about once a week. They make me extremely sensitive to light and usually cause severe pain. I often get so sick that I throw up. They happen more often when I'm tense or under a lot of pressure. For instance, I often come away from a visit with my ex-wife with one."

Example 2

* Vague statement of experience: "My marriage is disintegrating."
* Concrete statement of the same experience: "My husband is going around with other women, though he won't admit it. He never asks me to have sex though occasionally it 'happens.' He is verbally abusive at times, though he has never hit me."

In the spaces below, explore the experiences, that is, what you see as happening to you, related to three of your concerns or problems that might relate to the quality of your helping.

1. Vague. _____

_____

Concrete. _____

_____

_____

_____

2. Vague. _____

_____

   Concrete. _____

_____

_____

_____

_____

3. Vague. _____

_____

   Concrete. _____

_____

_____

_____

_____

_____

EXERCISE 24: Speaking concretely about your behavior

In this exercise, you are asked to speak about some of your behavior (what you do or fail to do)--first vaguely, then concretely. Choose behaviors that might affect your role as helper. Read the following examples.

Example 1

* Vague statement of behavior: "I tend to be domineering."
* Concrete statement of the same behavior: "I try, usually in subtle ways, to get others to do what I want to do. I get women to engage in sex even when they would rather not. I even pride myself on this. In conversations I take the lead. I interrupt others, good naturedly and jokingly, but I make my points. If a friend is talking about something serious when I'm not in the mood to hear it, I change the subject.

Example 2

* <u>Vague statement of behavior</u>: "I don't treat my wife right."
* <u>Concrete statement of the same behavior</u>: "When I come home from work, I read the paper and watch some TV. I don't talk much to my wife except a bit at supper. I don't share the little things that went on in my day. Neither do I encourage her to talk about what happened to her. Still, if I feel like having sex later, I expect her to hop in bed with me willingly."

In the spaces below, deal with three instances of your own behavior. Stick to describing behaviors rather than experiences or feelings. Try to choose situations and behaviors that are relevant to your interpersonal or helping style.

1. <u>Vague</u>. _____

_____

<u>Concrete</u>. _____

_____

_____

_____

_____

2. <u>Vague</u>. _____

_____

<u>Concrete</u>. _____

_____

_____

_____

_____

3. <u>Vague</u>. _____

_____

<u>Concrete</u>. _____

_____

_____

_____

_____

EXERCISE 25: Speaking concretely about feelings and emotions

        Feelings and emotions arise from experiences and behaviors.
Therefore, it is unrealistic to talk about feelings without relating them
to experiences or behaviors. However, in this exercise try to emphasize
the feelings. Read the following examples.

Example 1

* Vague statement of feelings. "I get bothered in training groups."
* Concrete statement of the same feelings: "I feel hesitant and
embarrassed whenever I want to give feedback to other trainees,
especially if it is in any way negative. When the time comes, my heart
beats faster and my palms sweat. I feel like everyone is staring at me."

Example 2

* Vague statement of feelings: "I feel unsettled at times with my
mother."
* Concrete statement of the same feelings: "I feel guilty and depressed
whenever my mother calls and implies that she's lonely. I then get angry
with myself for giving into guilt so easily. Then the whole day has a
pall over it. I get nervous and irritable and show it to others."

        In the spaces below, deal with three instances of your own
feelings. Try to focus on feelings that you have some trouble managing
and which could interfere with your role as helper.

1. Vague. _____

_____

    Concrete. _____

_____

_____

_____

_____

2. Vague. _____

_____

Concrete. _____

_____

_____

_____

_____

3. Vague. _____

_____

Concrete. _____

_____

_____

_____

_____

EXERCISE 26: Speaking concretely about experiences, behaviors, and
        feelings together

    In this exercise, you are asked to bring together all three
elements--specific experiences, specific behaviors, and specific
feelings--in talking about some personal concerns. Study the following
examples.

Example 1

* Vague statement: "I'm not as mature sexually as I'd like to be."
* Concrete statement: "I'm afraid of women, especially women who
come on strong, even women who are just plain assertive. My sexual
life consists almost entirely of phantasies and masturbation. In these
phantasies I am the dominant male and women make no demands on me. They
are submissive and are there just for my sexual needs. I'm ashamed to
say that I get a kick out of it. Sometimes I'm obsessed by thoughts like
this. For the present it seems to satisfy my sexual needs. Some women
are attracted to me, but I make excuses why I can't go out. I'm really
scared, but I hide it by being humorous. I intimate that I have a life
full of women someplace else. So I feel phony when I'm around women.
And I feel guilty when I take any kind of serious look at myself as a
sexual person. I try not to think much about it."

    Pick out the experiences, behaviors, and feelings in this example.

65

<u>Example 2</u>

* <u>Vague statement</u>: "Sometimes I'm a rather overly sensitive and spiteful person."

* <u>Concrete statement</u>: "I do not take criticism well. When I receive almost any kind of negative feedback, I usually smile and seem to shrug it off, but inside I begin to pout. Also deep inside I put the person who gave me the feedback on a 'list.' I say to myself that that person is going to pay for what he or she did. For instance, two weeks ago in the training group I received some negative feedback from you, Cindy. I felt angry and hurt because I thought you were my 'friend.' Since then I've tried to see what mistakes you make here. I've been looking for an opportunity to get back at you. I've even felt bad because I haven't been able to catch you. It's embarrassing to say all this."

Pick out the experiences, behaviors, and feelings in this example.

Next talk about two situations in terms of your own experiences, behaviors, and feelings. Again try to deal with themes that relate to your potential effectiveness as a helper.

1. <u>Vague</u>. _____

_____

<u>Concrete</u>. _____

_____

_____

_____

_____

_____

_____

_____

2. <u>Vague</u>. _____

_____

<u>Concrete</u>. _____

_____

_____

_____

_____

_____

_____

_____

_____

_____

_____

EXERCISE 27: Counseling yourself: An exercise in Steps A and B.

In this exercise you are asked to carry on a dialogue in writing with yourself.

Choose some problematic area of your life, one that is relevant to your interpersonal style and / or to your competence as a helper. First use basic communication skills to help yourself tell your story, next choose a high-leverage issue for more extensive exploration, and then work at clarifying it in terms of specific experiences, behaviors, and feelings.

Example

This example comes from the experience of a man in a master's degree program in counseling psychology.

He tells his story. "To be frank, I have a number of misgivings about becoming a counselor. A number of things are turning me off. For instance, one of my instructors this past semester was an arrogant guy. I kept saying to myself, 'Is this what these programs produce? Could this guy really help anyone?' I find the program much too theoretical. In a Theories of Counseling and Psychotherapy course we never did anything, not even discuss the practical implications of things with one another. I'm very disappointed. I'm about to go into my second year, but I've got serious reservations. From what others tell me, the program gets a bit more practical, but not enough. There's a practicum experience at the end of the program, but I need more hands-on work now. So I've started working at a halfway house for people discharged from mental hospitals. But that's not working out the way I expected either. There's something about this whole helping business that is making me think twice about myself and about the profession."

Response to self: "These disappointments lead to reservations. Which one is bothering you the most right now?"

Self: "It's hard to pick, but I think the halfway house bothers me most. Because that's not theoretical stuff. That's real stuff out there."

Response to self: "That's a place where real helping should be taking place. But you've got misgivings about what's going on there."

Self: "Yes, two sets of misgivings. One set about me and one about the place."

Response to self: "Which set do you want to explore?"

Self: "I feel I have to explore both, but I'll start with myself. I feel so ill prepared. What's in the lectures and books seems so distant from the realities of the halfway house. For instance, the other day one of the residents there began yelling at me when we were passing in the hallway. She hit me a few times and then ran off screaming that I was after her."

Response to self: "It sounds frightening."

Self: "It was terrifying. I wasn't ready for anything like that. I've been there a couple of months, but then no one has really helped me learn the ropes. I don't have an official supervisor. Since I help different people at different times, I sometimes get hints from them. I see all sorts of people with problems and help when I can."

Response to self: "You just don't feel prepared to do what you're doing. You work hard, but you still feel inadequate, because of lack of supervision and perhaps lack of focus."

Self: "I'm an independent person, but I'm too much on my own there. In a sense, I'm trusted; but, since I don't get much supervision, I have to go on my own instincts, and I'm not sure they're always right."

Response to self: "There's some comfort in being trusted, but without supervison you still have a what-am-I-doing-here feeling."

Self: "Sure. There are times when I ask myself just that: 'What are you doing here?' I provide day-to-day services for a lot of people. I listen to them. I take them places, like to the doctor. I get them to participate in conversation or games and things like that. But it seems that I'm always just meeting the needs of the moment. I'm not sure what the long-range goals of the place are and if anyone, including me, is contributing to them in any way."

Response to self: "You get some satisfaction in providing the services you do, but this lack of overall purpose or direction for yourself and the institution is frustrating."

Self: "Frustrating, irritating. I'm depressed. I'm down on myself and down on the people who run the house. It's a day-to-day operation that sometimes seems to be a fly-by-night venture. In meetings we don't really talk about the patients. We talk about incidents! I'm not sure the place has any philosophy or goals beyond warehousing and keeping the peace."

Response to self: "What do you do when things get so miserable?"

Self: "I begin asking myself questions. I ask whether it's just me. Maybe I don't have what it takes to be a good helper. I wonder whether the halfway house is typical of the kinds of institutions that deal with people in trouble. I ask whether there is as much incompetence in the helping professions as I see at the house . . . and at school, too."

Response to self: "What answers do you come up with?"

Self: "That's a good question. First of all, deep down I think that I'd make a good helper. Second, I challenge my own idealism. Maybe this is what the helping world is like. I spend too much time grieving over what is happening at school and at the halfway house. I need to figure out how to turn minuses into pluses."

This trainee goes on to do some work on possible blind spots and on a preferred scenario dealing with an idealist managing his life in two imperfact institutions.

1.   Review this trainee's responses to himself. What kind of responses did he use? How would you evaluate their quality? Did they get him someplace?

2.   Choose a problematic area that is important to you and on separate sheets of paper engage in the same kind of dialogue with yourself. Tell your story briefly, choose a high-leverage part of it, and clarify it in terms of specific experiences, behaviors, and feelings. Stay within Steps A and B of Stage I.

EXERCISE 28:   Managing resistance and other process problems

     As suggested in the text, there are two kinds of problems in counseling situations: the concerns clients bring with them and difficulties with the helping process itself. Resistance on the part of clients is one of these difficulties; it can take many forms. However, just as the three-stage model is designed to help clients manage their problems in living, so is it useful in helping you manage process problems such as resistance.

1.   Current scenario. Picture a client engaged in some form of resistance. Describe in some detail precisely what you see. What is the client saying and doing? What are your reactions?
2.   Preferred scenario. What would it look like if this form of resistance were to be handled? What would the client be saying or doing that he or she is not saying and doing now?
3.   Strategies. By brainstorming, come up with a list of strategies that would help you help the client manage this kind of resistance.

4.   Best-fit strategies. After brainstorming (not during), pick the strategy or strategies you think might be most useful.
5.   Evaluation. In your training groups help one another evaluate your work.

Consider the following example.

1. Current scenario. This client is showing resistance by not talking about her own behavior. She keeps describing the problem situation with her husband almost exclusively in terms of experiences and feelings. She blames him for her difficulties.
2. Preferred scenario. The client owns the problem with her husband, describing it in terms of her own behavior. She does not blame him.
3. Strategies. Here are some strategies that might help the client own the problem situation.
* Have her describe her preferred scenario, what her dealing with or coping with the indifferent behavior of her husband might look like.
* Reverse roles with her. Have her play the counselor and use her energies to get you to own the problem.
* Talk to her directly about the difficulties you are having in trying to help her. Tell her how help is possible only if she begins to describe the problem situation in terms of what she does or does not do.
* Walk her through an example of turning a nonowning statement into an owning statement. For instance, if she says: "My husband never talks to me about our relationship," say to her, "I am going to say what you just said a little differently: 'I would like to talk to my husband about our relationship. I haven't found effective ways of getting him to do so.'" Then have a discussion with her about the difference.
4. Best-fit strategy. The helper chooses the first strategy because he thinks that this will get the client oriented toward the future instead of the past and that it will indirectly handle the problem of owning without alienating the client.
5. Evaluation. What do you think about the helper's choice? What feedback would you give him? What would your choice be (include items not on the list)?

Summarizing

At a number of points throughout the helping process it is useful for helpers to summarize or to have clients summarize the principal points of their interaction. This has a way of helping clients redirect their energies and it places them under pressure to move on. At this stage of the helping process, this means moving on toward the kind of problem definition and clarification that leads to the development of new scenarios and the setting of goals. Summarizing can be an effective way of helping a client move from Stage I to Stage II.

EXERCISE 29: Summarizing as an instrument of problem clarification

This exercise assumes that trainees have been using the skills and methods of Steps I-A and I-B to help one another.

1. The total training group is divided into subgroups of three.
2. There are three roles in each subgroup: helper, client, and observer.
3. The helper spends about eight to ten minutes counseling the client. The client should continue to explore one of the problem areas he or she has chosen to deal with in the training group.
4. At the end of four minutes, the helper summarizes the principal points of the interaction. Helpers should try to make the summary both accurate and concise, keeping in mind that it is meant to help the client move toward the kind of problem clarification needed for goal setting. The helper can draw on past interactions if he or she is counseling a "client" that he or she has counseled before. At the end of eight or ten minutes, the helper should engage in a second summary.
5. At the end of each summary, the helper should ask the <u>client</u> to draw some sort of implication or conclusion from the summary. That is, the client is asked to take the next step.
6. After this the interaction is stopped and both observer and client give the helper feedback as to the accuracy and the helpfulness of the summary. The summary is helpful if it moves the client forward in the helping process.
7. This process is repeated until each person in the subgroup has had an opportunity to play each role.

Consider the following examples.

Example 1

It would be too cumbersome to print ten minutes of dialogue here, but consider this brief outline of a case.

A young man, 22, has been talking about some developmental issues. One of his concerns is that he sees himself as relating poorly to women. One side of his face is scarred from a fire two years previous to the counseling session. He has made some previous remarks about the difficulties he has relating to women. After five minutes of interaction, the helper summarizes:

> Helper: "Dave, let me see if I have the main points you've been making. First, because of the scars, you think you turn women off before you even get to talk with them. The second point—and I have to make sure that this is what you are saying—is that your initial approach to women is cautious, or cynical, or maybe even subtly hostile since you've come to expect rejection somewhat automatically."
> Dave: "Yeah, but now that I'm looking at it, I'm not sure that it's so subtle."
> Helper: "You also said that the women you meet are cautious

with you. Some might see you as 'mean.' Some steer clear of you because they see you as a kind of 'difficult person.' What closes the circle is that you take their caution or aloofness as their being turned off by your physical appearance."

Dave. "I don't like to hear it that way, but that's what I've been saying."

Helper. "If these points are fairly accurate, I wonder what implication you might see in them."

Dave: "I'm the one that rejects me because of my face. Nothing's going to get better until I do something about that."

Note that the client draws an implication from the summary ("I am the primary one who rejects me") and moves on to some minimal declaration of intent ("I need to change this").

Example 2

A woman, 47, has been talking about her behavior in the training group. She feels that she is quite nonassertive and that this stands in the way of being an effective helper. She and her helper explore this theme for about ten minutes and then the helper gives the following summary:

Helper: "I'd like to take a moment to pull together the main points of our conversation. You're convinced that the ability to 'intrude' reasonably into the life of the client is essential for you as a helper. However, this simply has not been part of your normal interpersonal style. If anything, you are too hesitant to make demands on anyone. When you take the role of helper in training sessions, you feel awkward using even basic empathy and even more awkward using probes. As a result you let your clients ramble and their problems remain unfocused. Outside training sessions you still see yourself as quite passive, except now you're much more aware of it. If this is more or less accurate, what implication might you draw from it?"

Client: "When I hear it all put together like that, my immediate reaction is to say that I shouldn't try to be a counselor. But I think I would be selling myself short. No matter what I do in life, I can't keep on being such a hesitant person. I have to learn how to take risks."

In the client's new scenario, she is a risk taker.

The feedback should center on the accuracy and the usefulness of the summary, not on a further exploration of the client's problem. Recall that feedback is most effective when it is clear, concise, behavioral, and nonpunitive.

STEP I-C: HELPING CLIENTS MANAGE BLIND SPOTS AND
DEVELOP NEW PERSPECTIVES

Challenging skills include information sharing, advanced empathy, confrontation, helper self-sharing, and immediacy. The purpose of these skills is to help clients get in touch with blind spots and develop the kind of new perspectives or behavioral insights needed to complete the clarification of a problem situation and move on to developing new scenarios and setting problem-managing goals. Challenging skills, then, do not represent behaviors that are good in themselves. They are good if they are instrumental in helping clients complete the process of problem clarification.

INFORMATION GIVING

As noted in the text, sometimes clients do not get a clear picture of a problem situation because they are not aware that they lack information needed for clarity. Information can provide clients with some of the new perspectives they need to see problem situations as manageable. However, giving clients problem-clarifying information or helping them find it themselves is not the same as advice giving. Furthermore, information giving is not to be confused with cliches or amateur philosophizing.

EXERCISE 30: Information and new perspectives

In this exercise you are asked to consider what kind of information you might give or help clients get that would help them see the problem situations they are facing more clearly. Information can, somewhat artificially, be divided into two kinds: (a) information that helps them understand their difficulties better, and (b) information about how they might handle it. In this exercise we are interested in the former. Consider the following example.

A young man in his last semester in college came to a counselor because he was extremely disappointed that he had been unable to get into graduate school in psychology or counseling. The college he was attending was the seminary division of a large university. He was a person of average intellectual ability. He had gotten as far as he had educationally because he worked extremely hard. He was leaving the seminary, while most of his friends were staying. A few of his friends were also leaving the seminary, but they had all been accepted into graduate schools. In his experience, then, most people were going on to some form of graduate education. He felt that he was a failure and that the world was shutting him out.
Information for new perspectives. In this case the counselor realized that the client had a number of misconceptions about education and about the relationship between education and successful employment. He shared with the client the educational "pyramid," that is the percentage of people in North America who attend primary school, the

percentage that graduate, the percentage who go on to high school, the percentage who graduate, and so on. Once the client saw this "bigger picture," he had a better context in which to deal with his own concerns. The counselor shared other information about on-the-job training. Since the client had been in the seminary in both high school and college, he had a very restricted view of the kinds of jobs there were in the world and the kinds of nongraduate training available to prepare for them.

Note that this information sharing session was not a form of advice giving nor was it a subtle way of telling the client that he didn't have a problem. Rather it challenged a blind spot and helped him develop the kinds of new perspectives that would enable him to set his own goals.

In the following cases what kinds of information do you believe might help the client see his or her problem situation more clearly? What blind spots might be challenged by new information? What new perspectives might information provide?

1. A man, 26, has just been sentenced to five years in a penitentiary. He is talking to a chaplain-counselor who has worked at the penitentiary to which the man has been assigned for the past ten years and who had been counseling the man during his trial. The man is deathly afraid of going to prison and has even talked about taking his own life. What kinds of information might help him put his problems in some kind of useful context?

_____

_____

_____

_____

_____

_____

2. A woman, 45, has learned that she has cancer and will soon undergo a mastectomy. She has been put in touch with a self-help group composed of women who have had this operation. She is now talking to one of the members of this group.

_____

_____

_____

_____

_____

_____

3. A woman, 28, has been raped and is talking to a counselor at a rape counseling center. She has not yet reported the rape to the police.

_____

_____

_____

_____

_____

4. A man, 34, comes for counseling because he fears he's an alcoholic. He's been drinking heavily for several years and recently has had some physical symptoms that he hasn't experienced before, for instance, blackouts. He has never known anyone who was an alcoholic.

_____

_____

_____

_____

_____

5. A man, 41, comes to counseling because he fears he is going crazy. He has a number of problems. His marriage has deteriorated in the past year or so. He and his wife relate poorly to each other. He sees his teenage son and daughter drifting away from him and he doesn't understand this. He is drinking more than he should. He feels depressed, gets out of it, and then feels depressed again. He has begun to steal little things from stores, not because he needs them, but because for some unexplainable reason it gives him a lift.

_____

_____

_____

_____

_____

6. Cindy, 23, has been bleeding internally. She is about to undergo a series of tests. She is very frightened and fears the worst. She has never been seriously sick in her life. She fears the doctors, the tests, the hospital. She has never even visited anyone in a hospital.

_____

_____

_____

_____

_____

7. Tim, 18, has been smoking marijuana for about three years. He is a fairly heavy user. He has recently received several shocks. His father died suddenly and his steady girlfriend has left him. He has developed fears that he has been doing irreversible genetic damage to himself by smoking pot. He is fearful of giving it up, both because he thinks he needs it to carry him over this period of special stress and because he fears withdrawal symptoms.

_____

_____

_____

_____

_____

8. Edna, 17, is an unmarried woman who is experiencing her third unexpected and unwanted pregnancy. The other two ended in abortion. She feels guilty about the abortions. She is thinking about keeping this child. For all her promiscuity she seems to know little about sex. She believes that men just take advantage of her.

_____

_____

_____

_____

_____

9. Maxine, 54, has suffered a stroke which has left her partially paralyzed on her left side and with speech that is a bit slurred. She is about to be transferred to a rehabilitation unit. She is depressed.

_____

_____

_____

_____

_____

_____

EXERCISE 31: Information you may need for developing new perspectives on your own problems

In this exercise you are asked to review the problem areas you have chosen to deal with during this training program. Choose two areas and ask yourself whether there is some kind of information that would help you understand your problem more thoroughly or put it into a better perspective. Consider the following example.

Example

A trainee, 30, has been married a little over a year. He has just quit work to start full time in school in a counselor training program. He is having trouble with his marriage. He is having second thoughts about quitting his job and entering the program. He has had no background in psychology previous to this. In college he majored in history. In doing this exercise, he came up with the following:

"What kind of information would help me see my problem situation more clearly?

* I need information about what job opportunities there are for people like myself with an M.A. in counseling psychology.
* It would be helpful for me (and my wife) to know more about what kinds of pitfalls exist normally for a couple in the first two years of marriage.
* I know vaguely that I'm supposed to be in a particular developmental period (the age-30 transition) with its own normative crisis. I don't know anything about that period of life in our culture and how what is known applies to me.
* I need more feedback on how I am doing in the training program. I am interested in knowing what my talents in this area seem to be."

Choose two areas you are working on and ask yourself what kind of information would help you see yourself and your problem situation more clearly.

Problem area #1: _____

_____

Information needed: _____

_____

_____

_____

_____

_____

_____

_____

_____

Problem area #2: _____

_____

Information needed: _____

_____

_____

_____

_____

_____

_____

_____

_____

ADVANCED EMPATHY

Advanced empathy, described most simply, means sharing <u>hunches</u> about clients and their overt and covert experiences, behaviors, and feelings which you feel will help them see their problems and concerns more clearly and help them move on to developing new scenarios, setting goals, and acting. Advanced empathy as hunch sharing can be expressed in a number of ways. Some of these are reviewed briefly below. Before doing the following exercises, however, review the section of advanced empathy in the text.

Some approaches to advanced empathy

* Hunches that help clients see the "<u>bigger picture</u>." Example: "The problem doesn't seem to be just your attitude toward your brother-in-law anymore ; your resentment seems to have spread somewhat to his fellow workers. Could that be the case?"

* Hunches that help the clients see what they are expressing <u>indirectly</u> or merely <u>implying</u>. Example: "I think I might also be hearing you say that you are more than disappointed--perhaps a bit hurt and angry."

* Hunches that help clients draw <u>logical conclusions</u> from what they are saying. Example: "From all that you've said about her, it seems that you are also saying that right now you resent having to be with her. I know you haven't said that directly. But I'm wondering if you are feeling that way about her."

* Hunches that help clients open up areas they are only <u>hinting</u> at. Example: "You've brought up sexual matters a number of times, but you haven't pursued them. My guess is that sex is a pretty important area for you--but perhaps pretty touchy, too."

* Hunches that help clients see things they may be <u>overlooking</u>. Example: "I wonder if it's possible that some people take your wit too personally, that they see it as sarcasm rather than humor."

* Hunches that help clients identify <u>themes</u>. Example: "If I'm not mistaken, you've mentioned in two or three different ways that it is sometimes difficult for you to stick up for your own legitimate rights. For instance . . . ."

* Hunches that help clients completely own their experiences, behaviors, and/or feelings, even though they may be expressing only partial ownership. Example: "You sound as if you have already decided to marry him, but I don't think that I hear you saying that directly."

<u>EXERCISE 32:</u> <u>Tentativeness in the use of challenging skills</u>

As noted in the text, challenges are usually more effective if they do not sound like accusations. Therefore, in delivering challenges such as advanced empathy, it helps to run a middle course between accusing a client and being so tentative that the force of the challenge is lost.

1. In the examples of the different kinds of hunches just outlined, underline the words or phrases that you think add tentativeness to the challenge.

2. Indicate whether you believe that a useful degree of tentativeness has been expressed.

3. List other ways in which you believe that tentativeness can be expressed (that is, other than the ways used in the examples).

<u>EXERCISE 33:</u> <u>Advanced accurate empathy--hunches about oneself</u>

One way to get an experiential feeling for advanced empathy is to explore <u>at two levels</u> some situation or issue in your own life that you would like to understand more clearly. One level of understanding could be called the surface level. The second could be called a more objective or a deeper level.

1. Review the material on advanced accurate empathy.
2. Read the examples given below.
3. Choose some issue, topic, situation, or relationship that you have been investigating and which you would like to understand more fully with a view to taking some kind of action on it. As usual, choose issues that you are willing to share with the members of your training group and try to choose issues that might affect the quality of your counseling.
4. First, briefly describe the issue, as in the examples.
5. Then give your present "surface-level" description of the issue.
6. Next, share some <u>hunch</u> you have about yourself that relates to that issue. Go "below the surface," as it were; get in touch with possible blind spots. Try to develop a new perspective on yourself and that issue, one that might help you see the issue more clearly so that you might begin to think of how you might act on it.
7. In some way suggested by your instructor share your examples with one or more members of your group and give one another feedback.

<u>Example 1</u>: A man, 25, in a counselor training group:

<u>Issue</u>: His experience in the training group is giving him some second thoughts about his ability and willingness to get close to others.

<u>Level 1</u>: "I like people and I show this by my willingness to work hard with them. For instance, in this group I see myself as a hard worker. I listen to others carefully and I try to respond carefully. I see myself as a very active member of this group. I take the initiative in contacting others. I like working with the people here."

Level 2: "If I look closer at what I'm doing here, I realize that underneath my 'hardworking' and competent exterior, I am uncomfortable. I come to these sessions with more misgivings than I have admitted, even to myself. My hunch is that I am fairly fearful of human closeness. I am afraid both here and in a couple of relationships outside the group that someone is going to ask me for more than I want to give. This keeps me on edge here. It keeps me on edge in a couple of relationships outside. There are a couple of members of this group that I am afraid of."

Now this trainee can talk to specific members of the group and discuss what he fears might be asked of him. This is a step toward handling his fear of closeness.

Example 2: A woman, 33, in a counselor training group:

Issue: Her experience in the group is making her explore her attitude toward herself. It might not be as positive as she thought. She sees this as something that could interfere with her effectiveness as a counselor.

Level 1: "I like myself. I base this on the fact that I seem to relate freely to others. There are a number of things I like specifically about myself. I'm a hard worker. And I think I can work hard with others as a helper. I'm demanding of myself, but I don't place unreasonable demands on others."

Level 2: "If I look more closely at myself, I see that when I work hard it is because I feel I have to. My hunch is that 'I have to' counts more in my hard work than 'I want to.' I get pleasure out of working hard, but it also keeps me from feeling guilty. If I don't work 'hard enough,' then I can feel guilty or down on myself. I am beginning to feel that there is too much of the 'I must be a perfect person' in me. I judge myself and others more harshly than I care to think."

She goes on to explore the kinds of "sentences" she says to herself about herself and the ways in which she might be judging her fellow trainees.

First, choose four areas, issues, or concerns in your life around which you might develop the kinds of advanced empathic hunches illustrated in the examples. Just choose the areas without spelling out the hunches.

a. _____

_____

b. _____

_____

c. _____

_____

d. _____

_____

    As in the examples, develop Level 1 and Level 2 (advanced empathic hunches) about yourself—your experiences, your behaviors, your feelings—in each area. Do this on separate sheets of paper.

EXERCISE 34: The distinction between basic and advanced empathy

    In this exercise, assume that the helper and the client have established a good working relationship, that the client's concerns have been explored from his or her perspective, and that the client needs to be challenged to see the problem situation from some new perspective or frame of reference. First review the material in the text dealing with advanced empathy. Then follow these instructions:

1.   In each instance, imagine the client speaking directly to you.
2.   In (a) respond to what the client has just said with basic empathy. Use the formula or your own words. "You feel...because..."
3.   Next, formulate one or two hunches about this person's experiences, behaviors, or feelings, hunches which, when shared, would help him or her see the problem situation more clearly. Use the material in the context section and what the client says to formulate your hunches. Ask yourself: "On what cues am I basing this hunch?"
4.   Then in (b) respond with some form of advanced empathy, that is, share some hunch that you believe will be useful for him or her. Share it in a way that will not put the client off.

Example

    Context: A man, 48, husband and father, is exploring the poor relationships he has with his wife and children. In general he feels that he is the victim, that his family is not treating him right (that is, like many clients, he emphasizes his experience rather than his behavior). He has not yet examined the implications of the ways he behaves toward his family. At this point he is talking about his sense of humor.

    Client: "For instance, I get a lot of encouragement for being witty at parties. Almost everyone laughs. I think I provide a lot of entertainment, and others like it. But this is another way I seem to flop at home. When I try to be funny, my wife and kids don't laugh, at least not much. At times they even take my humor wrong and get angry. I actually have to watch my step in my own home."

a. Basic empathy: _"It's irritating when your own_

family doesn't seem to appreciate what you see as one of your talents."

82

Hunch: The family wants a husband and father, not a humorist. (or)

His humor, especially at home, is not as harmless as he thinks.

b. Advanced empathy: "I wonder whether their reaction to you could be

interpreted differently. For instance, they might not want an

entertainer at home, but just a husband and father. You know, just

you."

1. Context. A first-year engineering graduate student (to counselor) has been exploring his disappointment with himself and with his performance in school. He has explored such issues as his dislike for the school and for some of the teachers.

Client: "I just don't have much enthusiasm. My grades are just okay--maybe even a little below par. I know I could do better if I wanted to. I don't know why my disappointment with the school and some of the faculty members can get to me so much. It's not like me. Ever since I can remember--even in primary school, when I didn't have any idea what an engineer was--I've wanted to be an engineer. Theoretically, I should be as happy as a lark because I'm in graduate school, but I'm not."

a. Basic empathy: _____

_____

_____

Hunch: _____

_____

_____

b. Advanced empathy: _____

_____

_____

_____

2. Context. This man, now 64, retired early from work when he was 62. He and his wife wanted to take full advantage of the years they had left. But his wife died a year after he retired. At the urging of friends he has finally come to a counselor. He has been exploring some of the problems his retirement has created for him. His two married sons live with their families in other cities. In the counseling sessions he has been somewhat repetitiously dealing with the theme of loss.

Client: "I seldom see the kids. I enjoy them and their families a lot when they do come. I get along real well with their wives. But now that my wife is gone . . . (pause) . . . and since I've stopped working . . . (pause) . . . I seem to just ramble around the house aimlessly, which is not like me at all. I suppose I should get rid of the house, but it's filled with a lot of memories—bittersweet memories now. There were a lot of good years here. The years seem to have slipped by and caught me unawares."

a. Basic empathy: _____

_____

_____

Hunch: _____

_____

_____

b. Advanced empathy: _____

_____

_____

_____

3. Context. A single woman, 33, is talking to a minister about the quality of her social life. She has a very close friend and she counts on her a great deal. She is exploring the ups and downs of this relationship. In the counseling sessions this woman comes on a bit loud and somewhat aggressive.

Client: "Ruth and I are on-again, off-again with each other lately. When we're on, it's great. We have lunch together, go shopping, all that kind of stuff. But sometimes she seems to click off. You know, she tries to avoid me. But that's not easy to do. I keep after her. She's been pretty elusive for about two weeks now. I don't know why she runs away like this. I know we have our differences. She's quieter and I'm the louder type. But our differences don't ordinarily seem to get in the way."

a. Basic empathy _____

_____

_____

Hunch: _____

_____

_____

b. Advanced empathy: _____

_____

_____

_____

4. Context. A man, 40, is talking to a marriage counselor. This is the
third time he has come to see the counselor over the past four years.
His wife has never come with him. The other times he spent only a
session or two with the counselor and then dropped out. In this session
he has been talking a great deal about his latest annoyances with his
wife.

   Client: "I could go on telling you what she does and doesn't do.
It's a litany. She really knows how to punish, not only me but others.
I don't even know why I keep putting up with it. I want her to come to
counseling, but she won't come. So, here I am again, in her place."

a. Basic empathy: _____

_____

_____

Hunch: _____

_____

_____

b. Advanced empathy: _____

_____

_____

_____

5. Context. A high school senior is talking to a school counselor about
college and what kinds of courses she might take there. However, she
also mentions, somewhat tentatively, her disappointment in not being
chosen as valedictorian of her class. She and almost everyone else had
expected her to be chosen.

Client: "I know that I would have liked to have been the class valedictorian, but I'm not so sure that you are supposed to count on anything like that. They chose Jane. She'll be good. She speaks well and she's very popular. But no one has a _right_ to be valedictorian. I'd be kidding myself if I thought differently. I've done better in school than Jane, but I'm not as outgoing or popular."

a. Basic empathy: _____

_____

_____

Hunch: _____

_____

_____

b. Advanced empathy: _____

_____

_____

6. Context. A college professor, 43, is talking to a friend, who happens to be a counselor, about his values. He is vaguely dissatisfied with his priorities, but has never done much about examining his current values in any serious way. From time to time the two of them talk about values, but no conclusions are reached. He is not married. Work seems to be a primary value.

Client: "Well, it's no news to you that I work a lot. There's literally no day I get up and say to myself, 'Well, today is a day off and I can just do what I want.' It sounds terrible when I put it that way. I've been going on like that for about ten years now. It seems that I should do something about it. But it's obviously my choice. I'm doing what I'm doing freely. No one's got a gun to my head."

a. Basic empathy: _____

_____

_____

Hunch: _____

_____

_____

b. Advanced empathy: _____

_____

_____

_____

7. Context. A man, 50, with a variety of problems in living is talking
with a counselor. His tendency has been to ruminate almost constantly on
his defects. He begins a second interview on this somewhat sour note.

    Client: "To make myself feel bad, all I have to do is review what
has happened to me in the past and take a good look at what is happening
to me right now. This past year, I let my drinking problem get the best
of me for four months. Over the years, I done lots of things to mess up
my marriage. For instance, like changing jobs all the time. Now my wife
and I are separated. I don't earn enough money to give her much, and the
thought of getting another job is silly with the economy the way it is.
I'm not so sure what skills I have to market, anyway."

a. Basic empathy: _____

_____

_____

Hunch: _____

_____

_____

b. Advanced empathy: _____

_____

_____

_____

8. Context. A divorced woman, 35, with a daughter, 12, is talking to a
counselor about her current relationship with men. She mentions that she
has lied to her daughter about her sex life. She has told her that she
doesn't have sexual relations with men, but she does.

    Client: "I don't want to hurt my daughter by letting her see my
shadow side. I don't know whether she could handle it. What do you
think? I'd like to be honest and tell her everything. I just don't want
her to think less of me. I like sex. I've been used to it in marriage,
and it's just too hard to give it up. I wish you could tell me what to
do about my daughter."

a. Basic empathy: _____

_____

_____

Hunch: _____

_____

_____

b. Advanced empathy: _____

_____

_____

_____

9. Context. The wife of this man, 35, has recently left him. He tried
desperately to get her back, but she wanted a divorce. As part of his
strategy to get her back he examined his role in the marriage and freely
"confessed" to both the counselor and his wife what he felt he was doing
wrong in the relationship. Before that, part of his problem in his
relationship with both his wife and others was a need to get the better
of her and others in arguments. He could never admit that he might have
been wrong.

Client: "I don't know what's wrong with her. I've given her
everything she wanted. I mean I've admitted all my mistakes. I was even
willing to take the blame for things that I thought were her fault. But
she's not interested in a reformed me! Damned if you do, damned if you
don't."

a. Basic empathy: _____

_____

_____

Hunch: _____

_____

_____

b. Advanced empathy: _____

_____

_____

10. A nun, 42, a member of a counselor training group, has been talking about her dissatisfaction with her present job. Although a nurse, she is presently teaching in a primary school because, she says, of the "urgent needs" of that school. When pressed, she refers briefly to a history of job dissatisfaction. In the group she has shown herself to be an intelligent and caring woman, but she tends to speak and act in self-effacing ways.

Sister N.: "The reason I'm talking about my job is that I don't want to become a counselor and then discover it's another job I'm dissatisfied with. It would be unfair to the people I'd be working with and unfair to the religious order that's paying for my education."

a. Basic empathy: _____

_____

_____

Hunch: _____

_____

_____

b. Advanced empathy: _____

_____

_____

_____

HELPER SELF-SHARING

Although helpers should be <u>ready</u> to make disclosures about themselves that would help their clients understand their problem situations more clearly, they should do so only if such disclosures do not upset and distract their clients from the work they are doing.

EXERCISE 35: Experiences of mine that might be helpful to others

In this exercise you are asked to review some problems in living which you feel that you have managed or are managing successfully. Indicate what you might share about yourself that would help a client with a <u>similar</u> problem situation understand that problem situation or some part of it more clearly. That is, what might you share of yourself that would help the client move forward in the problem-managing process? First consider the following examples.

<u>Example 1</u>

Trainee: "In the past I have been an expert in feeling sorry for myself whenever I had to face any kind of difficulty. I know very well the rewards of seeing myself as victim. I used to phantasize myself as victim as a form of daydreaming or recreation. I think many clients get mired down in their problems because they <u>let</u> themselves feel sorry for themselves the way I did. I think I can spot this tendency in others. When I see this happening, I think I could share brief examples from my own experience and then ask clients to see if what I was doing squares with what they see themselves doing now."

<u>Example 2</u>

Trainee: "I have been addicted to a number of things in my life and I see a common pattern in different kinds of addiction. For instance, I have been addicted to alcohol, to cigarettes, and to sleeping pills. I have also been addicted to people. By this I mean that at times in my life I have been a very dependent person and I found the same kind of symptoms in dependency that I did in addiction. I know a lot about the fear of letting go and the pain of withdrawal. I think I could share some of this in ways that would not accuse or frighten clients or distract them from their own concerns."

1. List four areas in which you feel you have something to share that might help clients who have problems in living similar to your own. Just briefly indicate the area.

a. _____

_____

b. _____

_____

c. _____

_____

d. _____

_____

2. Next, on separate paper make more extended comments in each area, comments similar to those in the examples.

EXERCISE 36: Appropriateness of helper self-disclosure

In this exercise you are asked to review the client situations presented in Exercise 34. In each case, ask yourself whether you feel that sharing your own experience might in some way help the client. Note that this does not mean that you would necessarily share your experience. You are being asked only to see whether you have some experience that might help the client see his or her problem more clearly. Consider the following example (which is the example used in Exercise 34).

Context. A man, 48, husband and father, is exploring the poor relationships he has with his wife and children. In general he feels that he is the victim. He feels that his family is not treating him right, that is, like many clients he emphasizes what others are doing to him rather than his own behavior. He has not yet examined the implications of the ways he behaves toward his family. At this point he is talking about his sense of humor.

Client. "For instance, I get a lot of encouragement for being witty at parties. Almost everyone laughs. I think I provide a lot of entertainment, and others like it. But this is another way I seem to flop at home. When I try to be funny, my wife and kids don't laugh, at least not much. At times they even take my humor wrong and get angry. I actually have to watch my step in my own home."

First of all assume that you respond with basic empathy/accurate empathy, as in Exercise 34. Then ask yourself whether you have any experience that might help the client see the problem situation more clearly. If so, then mention what this experience is.

My experience: A person who was trying to become close to me once told me that he found it difficult to get past my humor and make contact with me. I was startled and began to see how I was using humor to keep people at a distance. In my case, it was one way I controlled what happened in relationships.

Now review each case in Exercise 34 and see whether you have some personal experience that might help the client get a better grasp of his or her problem. On separate paper jot down what you think could be helpful if presented in the right way.

EXERCISE 37: Practicing self-sharing in counseling interviews

In this exercise, you are asked to try your hand at sharing your experience to help your "client" see his or her problem situation more clearly.

1. The training group should be divided into groups of three--helper, client, and observer.

2. The client should continue to discuss a problem situation with which the helper is familiar, that is, one that has been explored in terms of Stage I.

3. Spend between five and ten minutes in a helping session. If you are the helper, once or twice during the session try to share some experience of yours that you think might help the client. Be brief and focused. Present your experience in such a way as not to distract the client from his or her own concerns.

4. When time is up, the observer and client give the helper feedback on the usefulness of the disclosure.
   * How pertinent was it?
   * Was it brief and focused?
   * Did the helper present it in such a way as to keep the attention on the client's concerns?
   * Did the client make use of the helper's disclosure? Did it help make the problem situation or some part of it clearer?

Consider the following example (related to the example in Exercise 36).

Helper: "I don't use a lot of humor at home, but if I don't watch out, I can talk endlessly about sports. I think my family wants me to talk to them, but I also think they want me to monitor the amount of time I spend in sports talk. I've been wondering whether your wife and kids might have similar feelings about your humor."

Repeat this exercise until each member of the three-person group has had the opportunity to be helper.

CONFRONTATION

Confrontation is a skill in which you invite clients to examine discrepancies that they are perhaps overlooking and which keep them locked into problem situations. Review the material on confrontation in the text before doing these exercises. Note especially that confrontations are meant to be instrumental, that is, they are useful to the degree that they help clients develop the kind of new perspectives that serve to define and clarify problem situations. Furthermore, confrontations are meant to be descriptions rather than accusations. If they sound like accusations rather than invitations, they tend to elicit defensive reactions in clients.

EXERCISE 38: Confronting one's own strengths

One of the best forms of confrontation is to invite clients to examine strengths and resources they are not using but which could be used to manage some problem situation more effectively. The discrepancy is that the strength is there but is not being used or used as fully as it might. In this exercise you are asked to confront yourself with respect to your own unused strengths and resources. Consider the following example.

<u>Problem situation</u>. "My social life is not nearly as full as I would like it to be."

<u>Description of unused strengths or resources</u>. "I have problem-solving skills, but I don't apply them to the practical problems of everyday life such as my less than adequate social life. Instead of defining goals for myself (making acquaintances, developing friendships) and then seeing how many different ways I could go about achieving these goals, I wait around to see if something will happen to make my social life fuller. I remain passive even though I have the skills to become active."

Now consider four problem situations or parts of problem situations you have been working on.

1. Briefly identify the problem situation.
2. Describe the problem situation or some part of it in terms of some strength, ability, or resource you are not using or are not using as fully as you might.

1. Problem situation: _____

_____

_____

Unused strengths: _____

_____

_____

_____

_____

_____

2. Problem situation: _____

_____

Unused strengths: _____

_____

_____

_____

_____

_____

3. Problem situation: _____

_____

Unused strengths: _____

_____

_____

_____

_____

_____

4. Problem situation: _____

_____

Unused strengths: _____

_____

_____

_____

_____

_____

EXERCISE 39: Further self-confrontation

Most of us face a variety of self-defeating discrepancies in our lives besides the discrepancies that involve unused strengths and resources. We all allow ourselves, to a greater or lesser extent, to become victims of our own prejudices, smokescreens, distortions, and self-deceptions. In this exercise you are asked to confront some of these, especially the kind of discrepancies that might affect the quality of your helping or the quality of your membership in the training group. Consider the following examples.

Example 1

The issue. This trainee confronts himself on being controlling in his relationships with others.

Trainee: "I am very controlling in my relationships with others. For instance, in social situations I manipulate people into doing what I want to do. I do this as subtly as possible. I find out what everyone wants to do and then I use one against the other and gentle persuasion to steer people in the direction in which I want to go. In the training sessions I try to get people to talk about problems that are of interest to me. I even use empathy and probes to steer people in directions I might find interesting. All this is so much a part of my style that usually I don't even notice it. I see this as selfish, but yet I experience little guilt when I think about it."

Example 2

The issue. This trainee confronts her need for approval from others.

Trainee: "Most people see me as a 'nice' person. Part of this I like, part of it is a smokescreen. Being nice is my best defense against harshness and criticism from others. I'm cooperative. I compliment others easily. I'm not cynical or sarcastic. I've gotten to enjoy this kind of being 'nice.' I find it rewarding. But it also means that I seldom talk about ideas that might offend others. My feedback to others in the group is almost always positive. I let others give feedback on mistakes. Outside the group I steer clear of controversial conversations. But I'm beginning to feel very bland."

Now confront yourself in three areas that, if dealt with, will help you be a more effective trainee and helper.

1. The issue. _____

_____

Descriptive self-confrontation: _____

_____

_____

_____

_____

_____

_____

_____

_____

_____

2. The issue. _____

_____

Descriptive self-confrontation: _____

_____

_____

_____

_____

_____

_____

_____

_____

3. The issue. _____

_____

Descriptive self-confrontation: _____

_____

_____

_____

_____

_____

_____

_____

_____

_____

EXERCISE 40: The confrontation round robin: Confronting and responding
    to confrontation

    The purpose of this exercise is to give you the opportunity to
practice both confrontation and nondefensive response to confrontation.
The assumption is that you have begun to know the other members of your
training group fairly well.

96

1. Review the material on confrontation and effective response to confrontation in the text.
2. Choose partners. In a six-person group there will be partners A–B, C–D, and E–F. Partners A, C, and E (a) point out something they have noticed that their partners do well in the training group and then (b) challenge their partners in some way (for instance, by pointing out a strength or resource that is being underused).
3. The partners of the challengers, B, D, and F respond first with basic empathy to make sure that they understand the point of the challenge.
4. Then the partners briefly explore the area challenged in terms of concrete experiences, behaviors, and feelings.
5. The second partner, B, D, and F then become the challenger and the process is repeated.
6. If possible, each member of the training group should have an opportunity both to challenge and be challenged by every other member of the training group.

Example

Partner A: "In our group sessions, you take pains to see to it that other members of the group are understood, especially when they talk about sensitive issues. You provide a great deal of empathy and you encourage others, principally by your example, to do the same. Your empathy never sounds phony and most of the time you're quite accurate.

"However, you tend to limit yourself to basic empathy. You seldom use probes and you seem to be slow to challenge anyone, for instance, by sharing hunches that would help others see their interactional styles more clearly. Because of your empathy and your genuineness you have amassed a lot of 'credits' in the group, but you don't use them to help others make reasonable demands on themselves."

B's response: "You appreciate my ability and willingness to be empathic. But I am less effective than I might be in that I don't move beyond empathy, especially since I 'merit' doing so. I should work on increasing my challenging skills."

A and B then spend _a few minutes_ exploring the issue that has been raised.

IMMEDIACY: EXPLORING RELATIONSHIPS

As noted in the text, your ability to deal directly with what is happening between you and your clients in the helping sessions themselves is an important skill. Relationship immediacy refers to your ability to review the history and present status of your relationship with other members of your group (your "clients") in concrete behavioral ways. Here-and-now immediacy refers to your ability to deal with a particular situation that is affecting the ways in which you and another person are relating right now, in this moment.

Immediacy is a complex skill. It involves (1) revealing how you are being affected by the other person, (2) exploring your own behavior toward the other person, (3) sharing hunches about his or her behavior toward you or pointing out discrepancies, distortions, smokescreens, and the like, and (4) inviting the other person to explore the relationship with a view to developing a better working relationship. For instance, if you see that a client is manifesting hostility toward you in subtle, hard-to-get-at ways, you may: (1) let the client know how you are being affected by what is happening in the relationship (self-disclosure), (2) explore how you might be contributing to the difficulty, (3) describe the client's behavior and share reasonable hunches about what is happening (challenge), and (4) invite the client to examine in a direct way what is happening in the relationship. Immediacy involves collaborative problem solving with respect to the relationship itself.

EXERCISE 41: Immediacy in your interpersonal life

In this exercise you are asked to review some issues that remain "unfinished" between you and others outside the training group.

1. Think of people in your life with whom you have some unresolved or undealt-with "you-me" issues (relatives, friends, intimates, coworkers, and so forth).
2. Briefly indicate what the issue is.
3. Imagine yourself talking with one of these individuals face to face.
4. Be immediate with this person with a view to instituting the kind of dialogue that would help the two of you grapple with the issue that concerns you. Your immediacy statement should include (a) self-disclosure on your part (the issue and how it is affecting you), (b) some indication of how you are contributing to the difficulty, (c) some kind of concrete challenge in the form of advanced empathy or confrontation, and (d) an invitation to the other to engage in dialogue with you on this issue.
5. Remember that initial challenges should be appropriately tentative.

Consider the following examples.

Example 1

The issue. A trainee sees herself speaking to a friend outside the group. She is dissatisfied with the depth of sharing in the relationship. She is hesitant about revealing her own deeper thoughts, values, and concerns.

Trainee talking directly to her friend: "I'm a bit embarrassed about what I'm going to say. I think we enjoy being with each other. But I feel some reluctance in talking to you about some of my deeper thoughts and concerns. And, if I'm not mistaken, I see some of the same kind of reluctance in you. For instance, the other day both of us seemed to be pretty awkward when we talked a bit about religion. We dropped the subject pretty quickly. I'm embarrassed right now because I feel that I may be violating the 'not-too-deep' rule that we've perhaps stumbled into. I'm wondering what you might think about all this."

Example 2

The issue. A trainee is speaking about her relationship to her boss. She feels that he respects her but, because she is a woman, he does not think of her as a prospect for managerial training.

The trainee talking to her boss: "I think you see me as a good worker. As far as I can tell, you and I work well together. Even though you're my boss, I see a sort of equality between us. I mean that you don't push your boss role. And yet something bothers me. Every now and then I pick up cues that you don't think of me when you're considering people for managerial training slots. You seem to be very satisfied with my work, but part of that seems to be being satisfied with keeping me in the slot I'm in. I don't see you as offensively sexist at all, but something tells me that you might unconsciously think of men for training slots before women. Maybe it's part of the culture here. It would be helpful for me if we could explore this a bit."

Now write out three statements of immediacy dealing with people in your life outside the training group. Choose people and issues that you would be willing to discuss in the group.

1. The issue. _____

_____

_____

_____

Write out a face-to-face statement on separate paper.

2. The issue. _____

_____

_____

_____

Write out a face-to-face statement on separate paper.

3. The issue. _____

_____

_____

_____

Write out a face-to-face statement on separate paper.

<u>EXERCISE 42</u>: Responding to situations calling for immediacy

In this exercise a number of situations calling for some kind of immediacy on your part are described. You are asked to consider each situation and respond with some statement of immediacy. Consider the following example.

<u>Situation</u>. This client, a man, 44, engages in a great deal of second guessing with you. He tells you what he thinks you're thinking and feeling about him. He suggests goals and programs that he thinks you would want him to choose and engage in. You have tried to ignore this behavior, but finally you are letting yourself get angry. He has good verbal skills and sometimes you feel that you are fighting for "on" time with him.

<u>Immediacy response</u>: "Tom, I'd like to stop a minute and explore what's happening between you and me in our sessions. Something's bothering me that I should have talked about sooner. At times you try to read my mind, second guess what I might be thinking about you or what you should do. For instance, earlier you said: 'I know you think I'm too passive and you're probably right.' Often enough these are your ideas and not mine. When I say that I didn't say that, we get into an argument. You argue well. It's almost as if we've got a little game going. You second guess. I resent it and say nothing or let myself get caught in an argument with you. My bet is that our 'game,' if it can be called that, is not contributing much to our work here. That's my perception. I'd like to hear your side."

Now consider the following situations and form an immediacy response.

1. <u>The situation</u>. The client is a person of the opposite sex. You have had several sessions with this person. It has become evident that the person is attracted to you and has begun to make thinly disguised overtures for more intimacy. The person finds you both socially and sexually attractive. Some of the overtures have sexual overtones.

Immediacy response: _____

_____

_____

_____

_____

_____

_____

_____

2. <u>The situation</u>. In the first session you and the client, a relatively successful businessman, 40, have discussed the issue of fees. At that time you mentioned that it is difficult for you to talk about money, but you finally settled on a fee at the modest end of the going rates. He told you that he thought that the fee was "more than fair." However, during the next few sessions he drops hints about how expensive this venture is proving to be. He talks about getting finished as quickly as possible and intimates that that is your responsibility. You, who thought that the money issue had been resolved, find it still very much alive.

Immediacy response: _____

_____

_____

_____

_____

_____

_____

_____

3. The client is a male, 22, who is obliged to see you as part of being put on probation for a crime he committed. He is cooperative for a session or two and then becomes quite resistant. His resistance takes the form of both subtle and not too subtle questioning of your competence, questioning the value of this kind of helping, coming late for sessions, and generally of treating you like an unnecessary burden.

Immediacy response: _____

_____

_____

_____

_____

_____

_____

_____

4. You are a woman. The client, 19, reminds you of your own son, 17, toward whom you have mixed feelings as he struggles to establish some kind of reasonable independence from you. The client at times acts in very dependent ways toward you, telling you that he is glad that you are helping him, asking your advice, and in various ways taking a "little boy" posture toward you. At other times he seems to wish that he didn't have anything to do with you at all and accuses you of being "like his mother."

Immediacy response: _____

_____

_____

_____

_____

_____

_____

_____

_____

_____

EXERCISE 43:   Immediacy with the other members of your training group

1. Review the general directions for Exercise 42.
2. Read the example below.
3. On separate paper, write out a statement of immediacy for the members of your training group (or selected members if the group is large). Imagine yourself in a face-to-face situation with each member successively. Deal with real issues that pertain to the training sessions, interactional style, and so forth.
4. In a round robin, share with each of the other members of the group the statement you have written for him or her.
5. The person listening to the immediacy statement should reply with empathy, making sure that he or she has heard the statement correctly.
6. Listen to the immediacy statement the other person has for you and then reply with empathy.
7. Finally, discuss for a few minutes the quality of your relationship with each other in the training group.
8. Continue with the round robin until each person has had the opportunity to share an immediacy statement with every other member.

Trainee A to trainee B: "I notice that you and I have relatively little interaction in the group. You give me little feedback; I give you little feedback. It's almost as if there is some kind of conspiracy of non-interaction between us. I like you and the way you act in the group. For instance, I like the way you challenge others, carefully but without any apology. I think I refrain from giving you feedback, at least negative feedback, because I don't want to alienate you. I do little to make contact with you. I have a hunch that you'd like to talk to me more than you do, but it's just a hunch. I'd like to hear your side of our story, or non-story as the case might be."

Point out the elements of immediacy--self-disclosure, challenge, invitation--in this example. Then move on to the exercise.

Part Four

Stage II:
Developing New Scenarios
and Setting Goals

As we have seen, Steps I-A, I-B, and I-C of the helping process, including the telling of the story, focusing together with initial problem exploration, and developing new perspectives, result in the kind of problem clarification that prepares clients for problem-managing scenario development and action. This is the work of Stage I. In Stage II, new scenarios and goals play a central part. Everything done in the steps of Stage I paves the way for developing preferred scenarios in Stage II. Stage III deals with action, that is, getting a preferred scenario on line. A preferred scenario is a goal or a package of goals. A goal is what a client wants to accomplish in order to manage a problem situation more effectively. Goals are to be distinguished from the strategies used to achieve goals. New scenarios and goals deal with what is to be accomplished, while strategies for action deal with how a goal is to be implemented. For instance, if a person wants to stop drinking, then "a life without alcohol" is his or her new scenario or goal. He or she can accomplish this goal through a number of different strategies.

The following exercises assume that you have reviewed the material on goal setting in the text.

STEP II-A: DEVELOPING NEW SCENARIOS

Effective helping is related to the use of imagination. In this step you are asked to help yourself and clients develop a vision of a better future. Once clients understand the nature of the problem situation, they need to ask themselves: "What would my situation look like if it were better, at least a little bit better?"

EXERCISE 44: Developing new scenarios—pictures of a better future

In this exercise you are asked in your imagination to build better "futures" for yourself as a way of preparing you to help others develop new scenarios. Consider the following example.

Since most students do not operate at 100% efficiency, there is usually room for improvement in the area of learning. Luisa, a junior beginning her third year of college, is dissatisfied with the way she goes about learning. She decides to use her imagination to invent a new study scenario. She brainstorms elements that might be in that new scenario, patterns of behavior that are not in her current learning scenario. She comes up with the following list:

* I will not be studying for grades, but studying to learn. Paradoxically this might help my grades, but I will not be putting in extra effort just to raise a B to an A.
* I will be a better contributor in class, not in the sense that I will be trying to make a good impression on my teachers. I will do whatever I need to do to learn. This may mean placing more demands on teachers to clarify points, to allow discussions with peers, to give me more freedom to learn the way I learn best, and so forth.
* I will have in place a more constructive approach to writing papers. For instance, once a paper is assigned, I will start a file on the topic and collect ideas, quotes, and data as I go along. Then, when it comes to writing the paper, I will not have to try to create something out of nothing at the last moment. I assume this will help me feel better about the paper and about myself.
* I will be reading more broadly in the area of my major, psychology—not just the articles and books assigned, but in the areas of my interest. I will let my desire to know drive my learning.

Luisa goes on the draw up a fairly extensive list of the patterns of behavior that might have a place in her new scenario. Only when she has an extensive list does she address the task of evaluating and choosing the actual elements that she will work at to include in her preferred scenario.

1. Review the material in the text on developing new scenarios.
2. Just as Luisa created possible elements for a new scenario relating to her approach to study, so you are to brainstorm on separate sheets of paper possible new-scenario elements for two of the following topics. What would be the possible elements of a new scenario dealing with:

    * a relationship you would like to improve?
    * your relationship to your family?
    * the way you manage your time?
    * your use of leisure time?
    * the physical shape you are in?
    * your overall social life?
    * your job?
3. Use the following questions to help yourself develop elements for a new scenario:
    * What would the current scenario look like if it were better?
    * What new patterns of behavior would be in place? Consider only your own behavior.
    * What patterns of behavior would be lessened or eliminated?
    * What accomplishments would exist that do not exist now?
    * What would be fractionally better? What would be substantially

better? What would be dramatically better?
* Who are the exemplars, that is, what people are currently doing or accomplishing what you'd like to do or accomplish?

EXERCISE 45: New scenarios related to your own problem situations

In many of the exercises in this manual, you have been working on one or more of your own problem situations, especially those that might affect the way you help or counsel others.

1. Choose two of the problem situations you have been working on, ones that you have explored and clarified. Give a brief summary of these problem situations or some significant parts of them that you have clarified.

_____

_____

_____

_____

_____

2. On separate sheets of paper, brainstorm possible elements for a new scenario as you did in the previous exercise. What are some of the elements of a preferred scenario for each problem situation?

EXERCISE 46: Helping others develop new scenarios

In this exercise, you are asked to help one of the other members of your group develop new scenarios.

1. You need a partner for this exercise.
2. One partner takes the role of client and the other the role of the helper.
3. If you are the helper, ask the client to share a summary of the problem situation.
4. After having the client share his or her list of new scenario elements (the ones developed in the previous exercise), help him or her expand the list. Use probes to help the client tap his or her imagination more fully. Use the items on the client's list as jumping-off points. Develop the items more fully and expand the list.
5. After the exercise is over, get a new partner and change roles; that is, if you have been the helper, take the role of the client.

STEP II-B: HELPING CLIENTS EVALUATE NEW SCENARIOS

Once new-scenario elements, which, if implemented, will manage the
problem situation or some part of it more effectively, are clarified, they
need to be evaluated. For instance, new scenarios are more likely to be
implemented if they are specific.

EXERCISE 47: Making goals more and more specific

In this exercise you are asked to move from less to more explicit
scenarios. First, read the following example.

Context. Tom, 42, has been talking to a counselor about how poorly
he relates to his wife. She has refused to come to the counseling
sessions. Tom has stopped blaming her, has explored his own behavior in
concrete ways, has developed a variety of new perspectives on himself as
husband and father, and now wants to do something about what he has
learned.
Without having specific information about the issues Tom has
discussed, use your imagination to come up with four levels of
concreteness in a goal-shaping process that might apply to Tom's
situation. That is, choose four levels of concreteness (from a mere
statement of intent to a concrete and specific goal) that you think
someone in Tom's position might choose. Obviously, in an actual
counseling situation, you would be helping Tom shape his own goals. This
exercise deals with goals (what is to be done), not with action
strategies (how any specific goal is to be accomplished).

Level I: Statement of intent: "I've got to do something about my
marriage."

Level II: General objective: "I'd like to improve the quality of the
time I spend with my wife at home."

Level III: More specific aim: "I want to have better conversations with
my wife."

Level IV: Specific goal: "I'd like to decrease the number of times our
conversations turn into arguments or out-and-out fights."

Note that each level becomes more specific in some way. Note, too,
that Tom's specific goal is negative; he does not say what he'd like to
put in place of fighting. Now do the same with the following
situations. Since you do not know the specific issues the client has
been discussing, you will have to use your imagination. The purpose of
this exercise is to help you develop the ability to move from vague
statements of intent to specific goals.

1. <u>Context</u>. Linda W., 68, is dying of cancer. She has been talking to a pastoral counselor about her dying. One of her principal concerns is that her husband does not talk to her about her impending death. She has a variety of feelings about dying that well up from time to time such as disbelief, fear, resentment, anger, and even peace and resignation. She also has thoughts about life and death that she has never had before and has never shared with anyone.

Level I: Statement of intent: _____

_____

Level II: General objective: _____

_____

Level III: More specific aim: _____

_____

Level IV: Specific goal: _____

_____

_____

2. <u>Context</u>: Troy, 30, has been discussing the stress he has been experiencing during this transitional year of his life. Part of the stress relates to his job. He has been working as an accountant with a large firm for the past five years. He makes a decent salary, but he is more and more dissatisfied with the kind of work he is doing. He finds accounting predictable and boring. He doesn't feel that there's much chance for advancement in this company. Many of his associates are much more ambitious than he is.

Level I: Statement of intent: _____

_____

Level II: General objective: _____

_____

Level III: More specific aim: _____

_____

Level IV: Specific goal: _____

_____

_____

3. Context. Linda, 32, is married and has two small children. Her husband has left her and she has no idea where he is. She has no relatives in the city and only a few acquaintances. She is talking to a counselor in a local community center about her plight. Since her husband was the breadwinner, she now has no income and no savings on which to draw.

Level I: Statement of intent: _____

_____

Level II: General objective: _____

_____

Level III: More specific aim: _____

_____

Level IV: Specific goal: _____

_____

_____

4. Context. Nancy, 19, unmarried, is facing the problem of an unwanted pregnancy. She has a variety of problems. Her parents are extremely upset with her. Her father won't even talk to her. She lives at home and is attending a local community college. These living arrangements are now unsatisfactory to her. Since, for value reasons, she has decided against an abortion, she does not want to live out the remaining months of pregnancy in an atmosphere of hostility and conflict. She is upset because her education is going to be interrupted and finishing college has always been high on her list of priorities. She is unsure about her finances and resents being financially dependent on her parents.

Level I: Statement of intent: _____

_____

Level II: General objective: _____

_____

_____

Level III: More specific aim: _____

_____

Level IV: Specific goal: _____

_____

_____

109

5. <u>Context</u>. Julian, 51, a man separated from his wife for seven years, has just lost a son, 19, in an automobile accident. He (Julian) was driving with his son when they were struck by a car that veered into them from the other side of the road. Julian, who had his seat belt fastened, escaped with only cuts and bruises. His son was thrown through the windshield and killed instantly. The driver of the other car is still in critical condition and may or may not live. Now, ten days after the accident, Julian is still in psychological shock and plagued with anger, guilt, and grief. He has not gone back to work and has been avoiding relatives and friends because he finds "getting sympathy painful."

Level I: Statement of intent: _____

_____

Level II: General objective: _____

_____

Level III: More specific aim: _____

_____

Level IV: Specific goal: _____

_____

_____

6.   <u>Context</u>.   Felicia, 44, finds that her nonassertiveness is causing her problems. She is especially bothered at work. She finds that a number of people in the office feel quite free to interrupt her when she is in the middle of a project. She gets angry with herself because her tendency is to put aside what she is doing and try to meet the needs of the person who has interrupted her. As a result, she at times misses important deadlines associated with the projects on which she is working. She feels that others see her as a "soft touch."

Level I: Statement of intent: _____

_____

Level II: General objective: _____

_____

Level III: More specific aim: _____

_____

Level IV: Specific goal: _____

_____

_____

EXERCISE 48: Checking goals against criteria

A goal, in order to be fully a goal, must meet the following standards or criteria:

* It must be an <u>accomplishment</u>, an outcome, an achievement, rather than a program.
* It must be behaviorally <u>clear and specific</u>.
* It must be <u>measurable or verifiable</u>.
* It must be <u>realistic</u>, that is, within the control of the client, within his or her resources, and environmentally possible.
* It must be <u>adequate</u>, that is, if accomplished, it should in some substantive way contribute to handling the problem situation or some part of it.
* It must be in keeping with the <u>values</u> of the client.
* It must be accomplished within a <u>reasonable time frame</u>.

1. Return to the specific goals you have come up with in each of the cases in the previous exercise and see whether each of these criteria is fulfilled for each goal.
2. If the goal does not meet these standards, restate it so that it does.

Example

Tom's Level IV specific goal is: "I'd like to decrease the number of times our conversations turn into arguments or out-and-out fights."

* <u>Accomplishment</u>. "Number of fights <u>decreased</u>" is an accomplishment. A new pattern of behavior would be <u>in place</u>.
* <u>Clarity</u>. It is behaviorally <u>clear</u>. Tom can get a picture of himself not arguing or fighting.
* <u>Verifiability</u>. Since Tom has some idea of how often they fight per day or week, he can <u>verify</u> whether the number of fights has decreased. It would be better if he indicated how much of a reduction he was looking for.
* <u>Realism</u>. Tom cannot control his wife's behavior but he can control his own. If it takes two to argue or fight, then Tom, by controlling his own behavior in a variety of ways, can control arguing or fighting. The assumption is that Tom has the self-management skills and the emotional resources to   control himself and keep from fighting.
* <u>Adequacy</u>. It makes sense to suppose that a decrease in the number of arguments or fights will contribute substantially to the betterment of their relationship. However, stopping fighting leads to a void. What is to take its place?
* <u>Values</u>. It has to be assumed that taking the kind of unilateral action necessary to reduce the number of fights is in keeping with Tom's values, that he does not feel that he is merely "giving in."
* <u>Time frame</u>. Tom does not state a time frame. This needs to be added.

<u>Restated goal</u>: "I'd like to reduce the number of arguments or fights we have from an average of two per day to two per week. Each time I avoid fighting, I'd like to bring up some constructive topic, if possible."

Now review each of the goals you came up with in the previous exercise, apply the criteria, and, if necessary, restate each goal so that it conforms to these criteria.

EXERCISE 49: Establishing goals for yourself

In this exercise you are asked to relate the process of Exercise 47 to some of your own concerns or problems.

1. Return to Exercise 45 in which you developed new-scenario elements for problem situations you are currently working on.
2. Take these elements and see whether they are statements of intent, general objectives, more specific aims, or specific goals. If they are not specific goals, shape them so that they are.

Example

Area of concern. Jeff, a trainee in a counseling psychology program, has been concerned that he does not have the kind of assertiveness that he now believes helpers need in order to be effective consultants to clients. He is specifically concerned about the quality of his participation in the training group. He comes up with the following:

Level I: Statement of intent: "I need to be more assertive if I expect to be an effective helper."
Level II: General objective: "I want to take more initiative in this training group."
Level III: More specific aim: "In our open group sessions when there is relatively little structure, I want to speak up without being asked to do so."
Level IV: Specific goal: "In the next training session, without being asked to do so, I will respond to what others say with empathy. During our two-hour meeting, I will respond at least ten times with basic empathy when other members talk about themselves."

Jeff applies the criteria for effective goals to his Level IV statement:

* "This goal is an accomplishment, that is, a pattern of assertive responding in place."
* "It is clear."
* "It is quite easy to verify whether I have accomplished my goal or not. I can get feedback from the other members of the group and from the trainer."
* "I have the skill of empathy but do not use it often enough. I can summon up the courage needed to use the skill. Therefore, the goal is realistic."
* "Responding with empathy with some frequency will help me develop, at least in part, the kind of assertiveness called for in helping. In this sense, my goal is adequate."

* "This goal is in keeping with my <u>values</u> of being a good listener and of taking responsibility for myself as a trainee."
* "I believe that I can put this new pattern in place within three meetings. I see the <u>time frame</u> as reasonable."

Now do the same for four goals from new scenarios you are trying to develop with respect to your own problem situations.

EXERCISE 50: <u>Helping others set concrete and specific goals</u>

In this exercise you are asked to act as a helper/consultant to one of the members of your training group.

1. Get a partner.
2. Decide who is to be helper and who is to be client.
3. The client goes through the list of specific goals developed in Exercise 49. The task of the helper is to make sure that each goal fulfills the criteria for specific goals.
4. Get feedback from your client as to how helpful your interventions have been.
5. After the feedback session, choose new partners, with the helpers becoming clients and the clients helpers. Repeat the entire process.

STEP II-C: CHOICE OF AND COMMITMENT TO GOALS

In this step, counselors help clients make final choices of goals that will constitute their preferred scenarios and help them commit themselves to these goals.

EXERCISE 51: <u>Estimating your level of commitment to goals</u>

In this exercise you are asked to review the goals you are choosing to manage some problem situation with a view to examining your commitment. It is not a question of challenging your good will. All of us, at one time or another, make commitments that are not right for us.

1. Review the problem situation you have been examining and the goals you have established for yourself as a way of managing it or some part of it.
2. Review the material on choice and commitment in the text and then use the following questions to gauge your level of commitment:

* Are you choosing this goal freely?
* Is this goal one from among a number of possibilities?

* How highly do you rate the <u>appeal</u> of this goal?
* Name any ways in which it does not appeal to you.
* If there are some ways in which it does not appeal to you, how do you intend to manage this lack of appeal?
* What are your principal incentives for choosing this goal?
* How strong are these incentives?
* If this is an imposed goal, are there other incentives besides mere compliance?

3. Choose a partner from your training group.
4. With your partner review your principal learnings from answering the above questions.

EXERCISE 52: Reviewing the cost/benefit ratio in the choice of goals

In most choices we make there are both benefits and costs. Commitment to a choice often depends on a favorable cost/benefit ratio, that is, the benefits must outweigh the costs. Consider the following example.

In January, Helga, a married woman with two children, one a senior in college, and one a sophomore, was told that she had an advanced case of cancer. She was also told that a rather rigorous series of chemotherapy treatments might prolong her life, but they would not save her. She desperately wanted to see her daughter graduate from college in June, so she opted for the treatments. Although she found them quite difficult, she bouyed herself up by the desire to be at the graduation. Although in a wheel chair, she was there for the graduation in June. When the doctor suggested that she could now face the inevitable with equanimity, she said: "But, doctor, in only two years my son will be graduating."

This is a striking example of a woman deciding that the costs, however high, were outweighed by the benefits. Obviously, this is not always the case.

1. Divide up into partners, with one partner acting as client, one as helper.
2. Let the client review one or more goal from a cost/benefit perspective. The helper is to use basic communication skills and the skills of challenging to help the client do this.
3. After the discussion, each is to get a new partner, change roles, and repeat the process.

Part Five

Stage III:
Action: Turning Preferred Scenarios
into Reality

Stage II deals with <u>what</u> clients would like to accomplish in order
to handle problem situations. Stage III deals with <u>how</u> to do this.
It deals with action--helping clients develop strategies, formulate
plans, and implement these plans at the service of problem management.

STEP III-A: DEVELOPING ACTION STRATEGIES

There is usually more than one way to accomplish a goal. Clients
tend to choose a better strategy if they choose from among a number of
possibilities.

EXERCISE 53: Brainstorming strategies for action

Remember that clients sometimes fail to achieve goals, even realistic
goals, because their thinking on <u>how</u> their goals might be achieved is too
constricted. Brainstorming is a technique you can use to help clients
move beyond overly constricted thinking. Recall the rules of
brainstorming:

* Do not criticize any suggestion you come up with. Suggestions are to
be evaluated later.
* Quantity is encouraged. Forget about the quality of suggestions for
the time being.
* Piggybacking and combining suggestions to make new ones are both
allowed.
* Wild possibilities are also encouraged--"One way I could stop eating
and lose weight is to have my mouth sewn up."

Consider the following example.

Ira is a member of a group of people who have been identified as high-risk candidates for a heart attack. Some of his relatives have died relatively early in life from heart attacks; he is overweight; he exercises very little; he is under a great deal of pressure in his job; and he smokes over a pack of cigarettes every day. One of his goals is to stop smoking. He would like to stop smoking within a month. He comes up with the following list of strategies.

Brainstorming—Ways to stop smoking:

* stop cold turkey
* cut down, one less per day until zero is reached
* look at movies of people with lung cancer
* pray for help from God to quit
* use those progressive filters
* switch to a brand I don't like
* switch to a brand that is very heavy in tars and nicotine, one that even I see as too much
* smoke constantly until I can't stand it anymore
* let people know that I'm quitting
* put an ad in the paper in which I commit myself to stopping
* send a dollar for each cigarette smoked to a cause I don't believe in, for instance, the "other" political party
* get hypnotized; through a variety of post-hypnotic suggestions have the craving for smoking lessened
* pair smoking with painful electric shocks
* take a pledge before my minister to stop smoking
* join a professional group for those who want to stop smoking
* visit the hospital and talk to people dying of lung cancer
* if I buy cigarettes and have one or two, throw the rest away as soon as I come to my senses
* hire someone to follow me around and make fun of me whenever I have a cigarette
* have my hands put in casts so I can't hold a cigarette
* don't allow myself to watch television on the days in which I have even one cigarette
* reward myself with a fishing trip once I have not smoked for two weeks
* substitute chewing gum for smoking
* avoid friends who smoke
* don't buy cigarettes and therefore be put in the demeaning position of having to borrow them
* have a ceremony in which I ritually burn whatever cigarettes I have and commit myself to living without them
* suck on hard candy made with the new sweetener Aspertame instead of smoking
* give myself points each time I want to smoke a cigarette and don't; when I have saved up a number of points reward myself in some way

Now do the same with the four goals you devised for yourself in Exercise 49.

Goal 1: _____

_____

_____

_____

On a separate page, brainstorm ways of achieving this goal. Observe the
brainstorming rules. When you think you have run out of possibilities,
force yourself to think of some wilder possibilities.

Goal 2: _____

_____

_____

_____

Brainstorm ways of achieving this goal. Add wilder possibilities at the
end.

Goal 3: _____

_____

_____

_____

Brainstorm ways of accomplishing this goal. At the end, let your
imagination run wild.

Goal 4: _____

_____

_____

_____

EXERCISE 54: Helping others brainstorm program possibilities

As a counselor, you can help clients stimulate their imaginations to
come up with creative ways of achieving goals. Use probes based on
questions such as the following:

* Who can help you achieve your goal? What people are resources for you?
* What, that is, what things, what resources both inside yourself and
outside can help you accomplish your goals?

*   <u>Where</u>, that is, <u>what places</u> can help you achieve your goal?
*   <u>When</u>, that is <u>what times</u> or what kind of <u>timing</u> can help you achieve your goal? Is one time better than another?

1. The group should be divided into partners.
2. Decide which partner will be the helper and which the client.
3. The client will briefly summarize a concern or problem and the preferred scenario that he or she has decided on   as a way of managing the concern. If the preferred scenario is a package of goals, have the client pick one. Make sure that the client states the goal in such a way that it fulfills all the criteria for a behavioral goal.
4. Next, give the client five minutes to list as many possible ways of accomplishing the goal that he or she can think of. <u>Have the client write these down.</u>
5. Then help the client expand the list. Use probes and challenges based on the above questions.
6. Encourage the client to follow the rules of brainstorming
    *   Do not allow him or her to criticize the suggestions produced.
    *   Encourage your client to expand on the suggestions produced, to piggyback, to combine.
    *   When your client goes dry, encourage him or her to come up with wild possibilities.
    *   If the client gets stuck, "prime the pump" with a suggestion of your own, but then encourage the client to go on.
    *   Reinforce your client ("that's good; keep them coming"), not for "good" suggestions, but for sheer quantity.
7. When the trainer signals the end of the session, stop and receive feedback from your client as to the helpfulness of your probes and challenges. Remember the desired outcome is quantity not quality of strategies.
8. After a couple of minutes of feedback, change partners. If you were the helper, choose someone who had been a client. Repeat the process.

EXERCISE 55: <u>Rating program elements</u>

Brainstorming and other imaginative techniques help clients gather data for the program-development process, but in and of themselves they are not decision-making techniques. If brainstorming is successful, clients are sometimes left with more possibilities than they can handle. They may need help in choosing program elements that will work best for them. The strategies that have been brainstormed, including the wilder ones that have been "tamed" in one way or another, need to be rated in order to discover which will be most useful.

1. Take one of the lists you produced in Exercise 53.
2. Add any further possibilities that have come to mind since doing the list.
3. Give each possibility a number.
4. Review the following C-R-A-V-E criteria for judging the usefulness or the workability of any given program possibility or course of action.

<u>C</u> – <u>Control</u>: To what degree do I have <u>control</u> over this strategy including control over the <u>resources</u> needed to engage in it?
<u>R</u> – <u>Relevancy</u>: To what degree will this strategy or course of action lead to getting the goal <u>accomplished</u>?
<u>A</u> – <u>Attractiveness</u>: To what degree does this course of action <u>appeal</u> to me?
<u>V</u> – <u>Values</u>: To what degree is this strategy in keeping with my <u>values</u> and <u>moral standards</u>?
<u>E</u> – <u>Environment</u>: To what degree is this course of action free from major <u>obstacles</u> in the environment?

5. Use the grid on the next page to rate the strategies or courses of action you have discovered through brainstorming on each of the above criteria. Use a scale of 1-5. If a course of action scores very low on any given criterion, assign a 1. If a course of action scores very high on any given criterion, assign a 5. Use the other numbers for points in between. First consider the following examples.

Example 1

A man who wanted to quit smoking considered the following possibility on his list: "Cut down gradually, that is, every other day eliminate one cigarette from the 30 I smoke daily. In two months, I would be free."

<u>C</u> – <u>Control</u>: "This is something that is in my control and I have the 'guts' or resources to do it, though it might become much harder toward the end. Rating: 4."
<u>R</u> – <u>Relevancy</u>: "It leads inevitably to the elimination of my smoking habit. Rating: 5."
<u>A</u> – <u>Attractiveness</u>: "I very much like the idea of not having to quit all at once. Rating: 5."
<u>V</u> – <u>Values</u>: "There is something in me that says that I should be able to quit cold turkey. That has more 'moral' appeal to me. Gradually cutting down is for 'weaker' people. Rating: 3."
<u>E</u> – <u>Environment</u>: "No one will notice that I am gradually cutting down. And I'll have time to take a look at what pitfalls, such as friends who smoke, lie before me. Rating: 5."

Example 2

A young woman has been having fights with a male friend of hers. Since he is not the kind of person she wants to marry, her goal is to establish a relationship with him that is less intimate, for instance, one without sexual relations. She considers the following possibility: "I'll call a moratorium on our relationship. I'll tell him that I don't want to see him for four months. Then we can both reestablish a different kind of relationship, if that's what both of us want, at that time."

<u>C</u> – <u>Control and resources</u>: "I can stop seeing him. I think I have the assertiveness to tell him exactly what I want and stick to my decision. Rating: 5."
<u>R</u> – <u>Relevancy</u>: "Since my goal is moving into a different kind of relationship with him, stepping back and letting old ties and behaviors

Rating Program Possibilities (Courses of Action)

Possibility	Control, Resources	Relevancy	Appeal	Values	Environment
1.					
2.					
3.					
4.					
5.					
6.					
7.					
8.					
9.					
10.					
11.					
12.					
13.					
14.					
15.					
16.					
17.					
18.					
19.					
20.					
21.					
22.					
23.					
24.					

die a bit seems to make a great deal of sense. A moratorium is not the same as ending a relationship, though it may lead to it. Rating: 5."

A - Appeal: "The thought of not having to think about how to relate to him for a while and the thought of ending the fighting has tremendous appeal. I also like the idea of not just ending the relationship. Rating: 5."

V - Values: "I'm not comfortable with this kind of unilateral decision. On the other hand, I don't value having sexual relations with someone I've ruled out as a possible marriage partner. Rating: 4."

E - Environment: "My friends are going to ask me where David is, why I'm not seeing him. Some are going to question my decision. David may try to see me before the moratorium is up. There are a number of bumps in the environment, but they seem manageable. Rating: 3."

In rating your own program possibilities, you are not asked to make the kind of commentary that appears in the examples. Use the CRAVE grid to rate each course of action. Do not spend a great deal of time making the ratings. If for some reason you have difficulty making a rating or have some second thoughts about the rating you do assign, circle the rating and review it later with one of the other members of your training group. When you finish the exercise, you should have a good idea of which courses of action are the best-fit strategies for you.

EXERCISE 56: The balance sheet

The balance sheet is another tool you can use to evaluate different program possibilities or courses of action. It is especially useful when the problem situation is serious and you are having difficulty rating different courses of action. Consider the following example.

Background. Rev. Alex M. has gone through several agonizing months reevaluating his vocation to the ministry. He finally decides that he wants to leave the ministry and get a secular job. His decision, though painful in coming, leaves him with a great deal of peace. He now wonders just how to go about this. One possibility, now that he has made his decision, is to leave immediately. However, since this is a serious choice, he wants to look at it from all angles. He uses the decision balance sheet to do so.

The format of the balance sheet is on the next page. Alex uses it to examine the possibility of leaving his position at his present church immediately. Here are some of the things he finds:

* Benefits for me: Now that I've made my decision, it will be a relief to get away. I want to get away as quickly as possible.
    * Acceptability: I have a right to think of my personal needs.
    * Nonacceptability: I don't have a job and I have practically no savings. I'd be in financial crisis. Further, this course of action seems somewhat impulsive to me, meeting my own needs to be rid of a burden.
* Benefits for significant others: The associate minister of the parish would finally be out from under the burden of these last months. I have been hard to live with.

* <u>Costs to significant social settings</u>: Many of the best programs are not rooted in the church system but in me. If I leave immediately, many of these programs will falter and perhaps die because I have failed to develop leaders from among the members of the congregation. There will be no transition period. The congregation can't count on the associate minister taking over, since he and I have not worked that closely on any of the programs in question.

    * <u>Acceptability of these costs</u>: The members of the congregation need to become more self-sufficient. They should work for what they get instead of counting so heavily on their ministers.

    * <u>Unacceptability of these costs</u>: Since I have not worked at developing lay leaders, I feel some responsibility for doing something to see to it that the programs do not die. Some of my deeper feelings say that it isn't fair to pick up and run.

The Balance Sheet

The goal: _____

The program possibility or course of action in question: _____

The benefits from taking this course of action:

* For me: _____

    * The acceptability of these benefits: _____

    * Ways in which these gains are not acceptable: _____

* For significant others: _____

    * The acceptability of these benefits: _____

    * Ways in which these gains are not acceptable: _____

* For significant social settings: _____

    * The acceptability of these benefits: _____

    * Ways in which these gains are not acceptable: _____

The losses or costs from taking this course of action:

* For me: _____

    * The acceptability of these losses or costs: _____

    * Ways in which these costs are not acceptable: _____

* For significant others: _____

    * The acceptability of these losses or costs: _____

 * Ways in which these costs are not acceptable: _____

* For significant social settings: _____

 * The acceptability of these losses or costs: _____

 * Ways in which these costs are not acceptable: _____

My overall evaluation of this particular program possibility or course of

action: _____

  Note that this is just a sampling of parts of the balance sheet the
minister filled out. You are now asked to fill out the entire balance
sheet. Follow these directions:

1. Choose a problem situation which you have clarified and for which you
  have established a preferred scenario with at least one goal that
  meets the criteria for a workable goal.
2. Choose a goal for which you have brainstormed strategies.
3. Choose a major strategy or a course of action you would like to
  explore much more fully.
4. Identify the "significant others" and the "significant social
  settings" that would be affected by your choice.
5. Explore the possible course of action by using the full balance sheet
  outlined on the previous page.

  Note that the problem area, the goal, and the course of action in
question should have a good deal of substance to them. Using the balance
sheet to make a relatively inconsequential choice is a waste of time.
  Note also that the balance sheet can be used to help you make the
kinds of ratings called for in Exercise 50, especially if the course of
action is serious and you're not sure how to rate it.

STEP III-B: FORMULATING PLANS

  Many goals call for strategies that involve more than one simple
step. If there are a number of steps in a program, then it is important
to put them in some kind of order. What needs to be done first? What
needs to be done second? How many steps are there? When you answer
questions like this, you come up with a step-by-step plan including a
reasonable timeframe for implementing it.

EXERCISE 57: Establishing the major steps in an action plan

The major steps of a plan leading to the accomplishment of a goal are often called subgoals. Consider the following example.

Eliza, 38, a widow with two children in their upper teens, wants to get a job. In accomplishment terms, "job obtained and started" is her goal. However, in talking to a counselor, she soon realizes that there are a number of steps in a program leading to the accomplishment of this goal. In putting together a plan, she comes up with the following major steps or subgoals and puts them in "accomplishment" language, that is, in terms of the accomplishment to be achieved by the end of each step.

* Step 1: Job criteria established. She soon discovers that she doesn't want just any kind of job. She has certain standards she would like to meet insofar as this is possible in the current job market.
* Step 2: Resumé developed. In order to advertise herself well, she will need a high-quality resumé.
* Step 3: Job possibilities canvassed. She needs to find out just what kinds of jobs that meet her general standards in some way are available.
* Step 4: A "best possibilities" list drawn up. She needs to draw up a list of possibilities that seem most promising in view of the job market and the standards she has worked out.
* Step 5: Job interviews applied for and engaged in. This includes sending out her resumé. She has to find out whether she wants a particular job and whether the employer wants her.
* Step 6: Best offer chosen and job started. If she receives two or more offers that meet her standards, she must decide which offer to accept.
* Contingency plan. If the kind of job search she designs proves fruitless, she needs to know what she is to do next. She needs a backup plan.

Follow this same process in arranging a multi-step program to achieve one of your own goals.

1. State a goal you would like to accomplish in order to handle some concern or problem situation. For instance, choose one of the goals you set in Exercise 49.
2. Review the strategies (courses of action) you discovered during the brainstorming exercises.
3. Choose a major strategy.
4. As in the example above, outline the major steps or subgoals that must be accomplished if you are to achieve the major goal.
5. Review each subgoal with one of the members of your training group. Check to see whether each subgoal has the characteristics necessary for any kind of goal:
    * Is it an accomplishment in its own right?
    * Is it clear and specific?
    * Is it verifiable, that is, will you know that you have accomplished it?
    * Is it realistic, that is, is it something you can control and something for which you have the resources?

* Is it <u>adequate</u>, that is, is it a major step toward accomplishing the principal goal?
* Is it in keeping with your <u>values</u>?
* Have you established a reasonable <u>time frame</u> for achieving this subgoal?

a. Goal to be accomplished: _____

_____

_____

_____

_____

b. Now indicate the major steps or subgoals that are to be accomplished in moving toward the accomplishment of the major goal.

Subgoal #1: _____

_____

_____

Subgoal #2: _____

_____

_____

Subgoal #3: _____

_____

_____

Subgoal #4: _____

_____

_____

Subgoal #5: _____

_____

_____

EXERCISE 58: Formulating subplans for the major steps of your plan

    If a preferred scenario is complex, for instance, changing careers or doing something about a deteriorating marriage, the plan to achieve it will have a number of major steps or subgoals. Usually a divide-and-conquer strategy is called for. That is, a plan is needed for each critical subgoal. For instance, getting a new job, as we have seen in Exercise 57, has a number of major steps or subgoals. Each of these major steps, such as getting a resume into shape, calls for its own plan. In this exercise you are asked to pretend that you are the person in Exercise 57 who is looking for a job. Draw up a plan to accomplish each of the subgoals leading to getting a new job.

a. <u>Job criteria established</u>. How would you go about the task of laying out the standards you would like to see a job meet?

_____

_____

_____

_____

_____

b. <u>Resumé put in order</u>. What would you need to do to produce an effective resumé?

_____

_____

_____

_____

_____

c. <u>Job possibilities canvassed</u>. How would you go about finding out what kinds of jobs are available?

_____

_____

_____

_____

_____

d. **A "best possibilities" list draw up.** If your job canvass reveals that there are a number of possibilities, what would you do to draw up a list of the best possibilities?

_____

_____

_____

_____

_____

e. **Job interviews applied for and engaged in.** How would you go about applying for interviews and what would you want to do to plan for the interviews themselves?

_____

_____

_____

_____

_____

f. **Best offer chosen and job started.** If you received more than one offer, how would you go about choosing?

_____

_____

_____

_____

_____

EXERCISE 59: Formulating plans for your own subgoals

In this exercise you are asked to come up with ways of achieving each subgoal you set for yourself in Exercise 57.

1. Restate your principal goal: _____

_____

_____

_____

2. Now briefly restate each major step or subgoal in your overall plan together with what you plan to do in order to achieve each subgoal. Space is provided for 5 subgoals. Of course your plan might have more or less than 5.

Subgoal #1: _____

_____

Summary of plan for subgoal #1. _____

_____

_____

_____

_____

Subgoal #2: _____

_____

Summary of plan for subgoal #2. _____

_____

_____

_____

_____

Subgoal #3: _____

_____

Summary of plan for subgoal #3. _____

_____

_____

_____

_____

Subgoal #4: _____

_____

Summary of plan for subgoal #4. _____

_____

_____

_____

_____

Subgoal #5: _____

_____

Summary of plan for subgoal #5. _____

_____

_____

_____

_____

EXERCISE 60: Developing the resources needed to implement programs

     Counselors can help clients to develop the resources they need to
implement plans leading to the accomplishment of either goals or
subgoals. It is a mistake for clients to try to implement plans for
which they do not have the resources. In this exercise you are asked to
help clients develop the kinds of resources they need to pursue their
principal goals.

1. Mildred and Tom are having trouble with their marriage. They do not
handle decisions about finances and about sexual behavior well. Fights
dealing with these two areas are frequent. They both agree that their
marriage would be better off without these fights and they realized that
collaborative decision making with respect to sex and finances would be
an ideal.

a. What kind of resources do you think they need to involve themselves
in collaborative decision making with each other?

_____

_____

Summarize a plan that might help them develop these resources.

_____

_____

_____

_____

_____

b. What kind of resources do you think they need to make better decisions about money?

_____

_____

Summarize a plan that might help them develop these resources.

_____

_____

_____

_____

_____

2. Todd feels bad about his impoverished social life. He is now in his upper twenties and has no intimate female friend and no close friends of either sex. He feels lonely a great deal of the time. Some of the goals he sets for himself involve joining social groups, developing wider circles of acquaintances, and establishing some close friendships.

a. What kind of resources do you think he needs to develop in order to join and remain in some kind of social group?

_____

_____

Summarize a plan that might help him develop these resources.

_____

_____

_____

_____

_____

b. What are some resources you think he probably lacks but will need to establish some closer and even intimate friendships?

_____

_____

Summarize a plan that might help him develop some of these resources.

_____

_____

_____

_____

_____

3. Ruth Ann wants to start a food cooperative in her economically disadvantaged neighborhood in a large city. She gets together a small group of intelligent and interested people. They realize that many such ventures fail. You are a consultant to their undertaking.

What are some of the resources they need to develop in order to move into the work of establishing a cooperative?

_____

_____

Summarize a plan that might help them develop some of these resources.

_____

_____

_____

_____

_____

     It goes without saying that, as a counselor, you would not be coming up with plans for clients but rather helping clients formulate their own plans for developing needed resources.

EXERCISE 61: Developing your own resources

     In this exercise you are asked to review some of the goals you have established for yourself (for instance, the goals in Exercise 49) and the plans you have been formulating to implement these goals with a view to asking yourself: What kind of <u>resources</u> do I need to develop to implement these plans? For instance, you may lack the kinds of skills needed to implement a program. If this is a case, then "requisite skills <u>developed or improved</u>" becomes the goal of a resource-development plan.

1. <u>Indicate a goal</u> you would like to implement in order to manage some concern or problem situation in some way. Consider the following example. Mark has headaches that disrupt his life. "Frequency of headaches <u>reduced</u>" is one of his goals. "The severity of headaches <u>reduced</u>" is another.

2. <u>Outline a plan</u> to achieve this goal. Note the parts of the plan that call for resources you may not have or may not have as fully as you would like. Consider Mark once more. Being able to relax both physically and psychologically at times of stress and especially when he feels the "aura" that indicates a headache is on its way is part of Mark's plan. This part of the plan calls for resources Mark does not have.

3. <u>Indicate the resources</u> you need to develop. For instance, Mark needs the skills associated with relaxing. He also could benefit from learning how to increase alpha waves, the brain waves associated with relaxation, at times of stress. He does not possess either set of skills. Furthermore, since he allows himself to become the victim of stressful thoughts, he also needs some kind of thought-control skills.

4. <u>Summarize a plan</u> that would enable you to develop some of these resources. Mark enrolls in two programs. In one he learns the skills of systematic relaxation and skills related to controlling self-defeating thoughts. In the other, a biofeedback program, he learns how to increase and maintain a high level of alpha waves, especially at times of stress. Fortified with these skills, he is now ready to apply them to a headache-reduction program.

<u>Problem situation #1</u>

a. Your goal: _____

_____

_____

b. Indicate the part of the plan that calls for skills or other resources you do not presently have.

_____

_____

_____

c. Indicate concretely the skills or other resources you would like to develop. Since the development of resources is a goal, your statement should have the characteristics of effective goals.

_____

_____

_____

_____

_____

d. Summarize a plan that can help you develop the resources you need.

_____

_____

_____

_____

_____

Problem situation #2

a. Your goal: _____

_____

_____

b. Indicate the part of your plan that calls for skills or other resources you do not presently have.

_____

_____

_____

c. Indicate concretely the skill or other resource you would like to develop. Since resource development is a subgoal, what you write should have the characteristics of a workable goal.

_____

_____

_____

d. Summarize a plan that can help you develop the resources you need.

_____

_____

_____

_____

_____

_____

STEP III-C: ACTION--IMPLEMENTING PROGRAMS

Once a workable plan has been developed to implement a goal or a subgoal, clients must act, they must implement the plan. There are a number of things you can do to help them act. You can help clients become effective tacticians "out there."   In this task, tactics, is the focus. Webster's Seventh New Collegiate Dictionary defines tactics in its military sense as "the science and art of disposing and maneuvering forces in combat." It is not a bad definition since at times the work of implementing programs resembles combat. However, tactics is also defined as "the art or skill of employing available means to accomplish an end [goal]." When clients are "out there" they are more likely to implement programs (strategy) if they can adapt themselves and their programs to changing conditions.

EXERCISE 62: Force-field analysis--identifying, facilitating, and restraining forces in implementing plans

In this exercise you are asked to identify forces "in the field" that might help clients implement programs and forces that might keep clients from implementing programs. The former are called "facilitating forces" and the latter "restraining forces." The use of force-field analysis to prepare for action is an application of the adage "forewarned is forearmed."

1. Review a goal or subgoal and the plan you have formulated to accomplish it.
2. Picture yourself "in the field" actually trying to implement the steps of the plan.

3. Identify the principal forces that are helping you reach your goal or subgoal.
4. Identify the principal forces that are hindering you from reaching your goal or subgoal.

Example

Martina wants to stop smoking. She has formulated a step-by-step plan for doing so. Before taking the first step, she uses force-field analysis to identify facilitating and restraining forces in her everyday life.

Some of the facilitating forces identified by Martina:

*   my own pride
*   the satisfaction of knowing I'm keeping a promise I've made to myself
*   the excitement of a new program, the very "newness" of it
*   the support and encouragement of my husband and my children
*   the support of two close friends who are also quitting
*   the good feeling of having that "gunk" out of my system
*   the money saved and put aside for more reasonable pleasures
*   the ability to jog without feeling I'm going to die

Some of the restraining forces identified by Martina:

*   the craving to smoke that I take with me everywhere
*   seeing other people smoke
*   danger times: when I get nervous, after meals, when I feel depressed and discouraged, when I sit and read the paper, when I have a cup of coffee, at night watching television
*   being offered cigarettes by friends
*   when the novelty of the program wears off (and that could be fairly soon)
*   increased appetite for food and the possibility of putting on weight
*   my tendency to rationalize
*   the fact that I've tried to stop smoking several times before and have never succeeded

Now do the same for two goals or subgoals you would like to accomplish.

Situation #1

a. A goal or subgoal you want to accomplish:

_____

_____

_____

b. Picture yourself in the process of implementing the plan formulated to achieve the goal.

c. List the facilitating forces you see "out there" that are helping or could help you to carry out the plan.

_____

_____

_____

_____

_____

_____

_____

d. List the restraining forces at work hindering you from carrying out the plan.

_____

_____

_____

_____

_____

_____

_____

_____

_____

Situation #2

a. A goal or subgoal you want to accomplish.

_____

_____

_____

b. Picture yourself in the process of implementing a plan for accomplishing your goal.

_____

_____

_____

_____

_____

_____

c. List the facilitating forces that could help you to implement the plan.

_____

_____

_____

_____

_____

_____

d. List the restraining forces that might hinder you from implementing the plan.

_____

_____

_____

_____

_____

_____

EXERCISE 63: Bolstering facilitating forces

Once you have identified the principal facilitating and restraining forces, you can determine how to bolster critical facilitating forces and neutralize critical restraining forces. In this exercise you are asked to devise ways of bolstering critical facilitating forces.

1. Identify facilitating forces (a) which you see as capable of making a difference in the implementation of a program and (b) which you believe you have the resources to strengthen.
2. Formulate a plan for strengthening one or more critical facilitating forces. Choose facilitating forces that have a high probability of making a difference in the field.

Example

Klaus is an alcoholic who wants to stop drinking. He joins Alcoholics Anonymous. During a meeting he is given the names and telephone numbers of two people whom he is told he may call at any time of the day or night if he feels he needs help. He sees this as a critical facilitating force--just knowing that help is around the corner when he needs it.

He wants to strengthen this facilitating force.
* First of all, since he sees being able to get help anytime as a kind of dependency, he talks out the negative feelings he has about being dependent in this way. In talking, he soon realizes that it is a temporary form of dependency and that it is instrumental in achieving an important goal, developing a pattern of sobriety.
* Second, he calls the numbers a couple of times when he is not in trouble just to get the feel of doing so.
* He puts the numbers in his wallet, he memorizes them, and he puts them a piece of paper and carries them in a medical bracelet which tells people who might find him drunk that he is an alcoholic trying to overcome his problem.
* He calls the numbers a couple of times when the craving for alcohol is high and his spirits are low. That is, he gets used to it as a temporary resource.

Situation #1

a. Briefly describe one or two key facilitating forces from Situation #1 in Exercise 62 that you would like to strengthen.

_____

_____

_____

_____

b. Indicate how you would like to go about strengthening these key facilitating forces. What do you plan to do?

_____

_____

_____

_____

_____

_____

Situation #2

a. Briefly indicate one or two key facilitating forces from Situation #2 in Exercise 62 that you would like to strengthen.

_____

_____

_____

_____

b. Briefly indicate how you would like to go about strengthening these key facilitating forces.

_____

_____

_____

_____

_____

EXERCISE 64: Neutralizing or reducing the strength of restraining forces

Sometimes, though not always, it is helpful to try to neutralize or reduce the strength of critical restraining forces.

1. Identify critical restraining forces from your list in Exercise 57, that is, restraining forces (a) which, if neutralized or reduced, would make a significant difference in the implementation of your plan and (b) which you feel you have the ability to neutralize or reduce.
2. Formulate a plan for neutralizing or reducing these restraining forces.

Example

Ingrid is on welfare, but she has a goal of getting a job. Part of her plan is to apply for and go to job interviews. However, she ends up missing a number of the interviews. By examining her behavior, she learns that there are at least two critical restraining forces. One is that she has a poor self-image; she thinks she looks ugly and that the interviewer won't give her a fair chance simply because of her looks. Another is that at the last moment she thinks of a number of "important" tasks that must be done--for instance, visiting her ailing mother--before she can do anything else. She does these tasks instead of going to the interview.

How might Ingrid handle the problem of feeling ashamed of her looks?

_____

_____

_____

_____

_____

How might Ingrid handle the problem of putting "important" tasks ahead of going to job interviews?

_____

_____

_____

_____

_____

Situation #1

a. Briefly indicate one or two critical restraining forces that you identified in Exercise 62 and which you see as critical.

_____

_____

_____

_____

b. What might you do to neutralize or reduce these restraining forces?

_____

_____

_____

_____

_____

Situation #2

a. Briefly indicate one or two key restraining forces that you
identified in Exercise 62 and which you see as critical.

_____

_____

_____

_____

b. What might you be able to do to neutralize or reduce these
restraining forces?

_____

_____

_____

_____

_____

EXERCISE 65: Identifying obstacles to program implementation--telling
    your program implementation "story"

     As we have suggested in an earlier exercise, "forewarned is
forearmed" in the implementation of any plan. One way of identifying
potential pitfalls is the force-field analysis method seen in previous
exercises. Another way is to tell yourself the "story" of what you will
encounter as you implement a program.

1. Either with yourself or with one of the members of your training
    group, begin telling the story of what your effort at implementing
    some program or subprogram will look like.
2. As you tell the story, jot down the pitfalls or snags you see
    yourself encountering along the way. Some pitfalls involve inertia,

that is, not starting some step of your plan; others involve <u>entropy</u>, that is, allowing the plan to fall apart over time.
3. Design some kind of subprogram to handle any significant snag or pitfall you see yourself encountering.

<u>Example</u>

Justin has a supervisor at work who, he feels, does not like him. He says that she gives him the worst jobs, asks him to put in overtime when he would rather go home, and talks to him in demeaning ways. In the problem exploration phase of counseling, he discovered that he probably reinforces this tendency in her by buckling under, by giving signs that he feels hurt but helpless, and by failing to challenge her in any direct way. He feels so miserable at work that he wants to do something about it. One option is to move to a different department, but to do so he must have the recommendation of his immediate supervisor. Another possibility is to quit and get a job elsewhere, but the present state of the economy makes that possibility remote. A third option is to deal with his supervisor more directly. He sets goals related to this third option.

One goal is to seek out an interview with his supervisor and tell her in a strong but nonpunitive way his side of the story and how he feels about it. The counselor asks him to begin spelling out the "story" of his implementation of the program to achieve that goal. Some of the things he says are:

* "I see myself asking her for an appointment. I see myself hesitating to do so because she might answer me in a sarcastic way. Also others are usually around and she might embarrass me and they will want to know what's going on, why I want to see her, and all that. . . ."

* "I see myself sitting in her office. Instead of being firm and straightforward, I'm tongue-tied and apologetic. I forget some of the key points I want to make. I let her brush off some of my complaints and in general let her control the interaction. . . ."

How can he <u>prepare</u> himself to handle the obstacles or snags he sees in his first statement? Then what could he do <u>in the situation itself</u>?

_____

_____

_____

_____

_____

How can he <u>prepare</u> himself to handle the pitfalls mentioned in his second statement? What could he do <u>in the situation itself</u>?

_____

_____

_____

_____

_____

Situation #1

Consider some plan or part of a plan you want to implement. In your
mind's eye see yourself moving through the steps of the plan. What
obstacles or snags do you encounter? Jot them down.

Obstacles: _____

_____

_____

_____

_____

a. Indicate how you might _prepare_ yourself to handle a significant
obstacle or pitfall and what you might do _in the situation itself_ to
handle it.

_____

_____

_____

_____

_____

_____

Situation #2

Consider another plan or part of a plan you want to implement. In your
mind's eye see yourself moving through the steps of the plan. What
obstacles or snags do you encounter? Jot them down.

Obstacles: _____

_____

_____

_____

a. Indicate how you might <u>prepare</u> yourself to handle a significant obstacle and what you might do <u>in the situation itself</u> to handle it.

_____

_____

_____

_____

_____

_____

EXERCISE 66:   The principles of behavior: Learning from program failures

In your text review the principles of behavior as they apply to the implementation of programs. It seems that many programs fail because people ignore or misuse such principles and procedures as reinforcement, extinction, punishment, shaping, and avoidance. In this exercise you are asked to review some program failures. You are asked to analyze these failures in terms of these principles of behavior.

* <u>Reinforcement</u>. Were there sufficient rewards or incentives for engaging in the program itself and in each of the steps of the program? <u>Example</u>: Corina wanted to graduate from college, but she never learned how to find rewards in studying. Each time she sat down with a text or a written assignment, she was in agony. Sheer "will power" got her through one and a half years of college. But it became too much for her and she quit.

What incentives might she have developed?   _____

_____

_____

_____

* <u>Punishment</u>. Was punishment misused as a motivator? <u>Example</u>: Perry was trying to lose weight. Whenever he ate more that his diet called for he punished himself by calling off some social engagement he enjoyed. This disrupted his social life, punished his friends, and made him feel isolated. When he felt isolated, he tended to compensate by eating.

What might he have done?   _____

_____

144

* <u>Extinction</u>.   Were the effects of extinction ignored?
Example: Lily wanted to read more serious books than her usual paperback
novels. She realized that at first she would probably not find that kind
of reading as rewarding (exciting) as she found pulp novels. She neither
rewarded herself when she did read a serious book nor did she punish
herself when she failed to read a serious book that she had intended to
read. At the end of a year she found she had read only one serious book
and part of a second.

What might she have done?   _____

_____

_____

_____

* <u>Shaping</u>. Was the program poorly shaped in terms of sheer amount to be
done and in terms of the size of the steps of the program?
Example. Till's doctor told him that he was prime material for a
coronary. He was overweight, he smoked heavily, he drank too much, he
did not exercise, and he did not manage the stress of his job or homelife
well. Till was scared by what the doctor said. He stopped smoking, he
went on a crash diet. He started a rather vigorous exercise program. He
became rather bland at work and at home. He became very depressed and in
a few weeks went back to his old style of living.

What might he have done?   _____

_____

_____

_____

* <u>Avoidance</u>. Were there more rewards for not engaging in the program or
any part of it than for engaging in the program?
Example. Gretchen and her husband Al said that they wanted to talk out
problems between them as they came up instead of saving up negative
feelings until they burst forth in a game of "uproar." However, whenever
one of them did something that annoyed the other, "forgetting it this
time" seemed more rewarding, or at least less painful, than talking it
out. They continued to have their periodic outbursts.

What might they have done?   _____

_____

_____

EXERCISE 67: Using the principles of behavior to bolster your
              participation in programs

     In this exercise you are asked to use the principles of behavior to
bolster programs you are currently engaged in or are about to undertake.

Situation #1

Briefly describe the goal or subgoal you are trying to achieve and the
principal elements of the plan you have formulated to reach your goal.

_____

_____

_____

_____

a. How can you use the principle of reinforcement to raise the
probability of your engaging effectively in the program? What kinds of
incentives will keep you working at your plan?

_____

_____

_____

b. How can you apply what you know about punishment, that is,
self-discipline, in a way that will raise the probability of your
carrying out your plan?

_____

_____

_____

c. How can you apply the principle of extinction in a way that will
raise the probability of your sticking to the plan?

_____

_____

_____

d. How can you use what you know about <u>shaping</u> to raise the probability that you will move efficiently through your plan?

_____

_____

_____

e. How can you use what you know about <u>avoidance</u> to help yourself engage in your plan as fully as possible?

_____

_____

_____

Situation #2

Briefly describe another goal or subgoal you are trying to achieve and the principal elements of the plan you have designed to achieve it.

_____

_____

_____

_____

a. How might you use <u>reinforcement</u> to strengthen your participation in the plan? What <u>incentives</u> will work best for you?

_____

_____

_____

b. How might you use facilitative self-punishment or self-discipline to strengthen your participation in the plan?

_____

_____

_____

c. How might you use <u>extinction</u> to strengthen your participation in the plan?

_____

d. How might you use <u>shaping</u> to strengthen your participation in your plan?

_____

_____

_____

e. How might you use what you know about <u>avoidance</u> to strengthen your participation in your plan?

_____

_____

_____

<u>EXERCISE 68</u>: <u>Monitoring and evaluating the implementation of plans</u>

One of the main reasons problem-management programs fail is that they are not monitored. Participation in a program slacks off sometimes without even being noticed. This means that monitoring has not been built into the program itself.

In this exercise you are asked to examine a program in which you are currently engaged and to ask yourself some monitoring questions. These questions are:

1. Are you participating or not?
    <u>Client</u>: "I checked with the doctor and set up a reasonable diet, but to tell the truth, I haven't started it yet. I've been more or less just trying to cut down on what I eat?"
    <u>Counselor</u>: "With what kind of results?"
    <u>Client</u>: "I'm not sure. I haven't really checked."

2. If you are participating, how fully are you participating? What are you doing? What are you failing to do?
    Todd and Sue had agreed to talk out petty annoyances with each other instead of saving them. Sue said that she was doing this except when the annoyance included feelings of hurt. Todd said that he was doing this except when he felt his annoyance was too petty to discuss. Therefore, neither was participating <u>fully</u> in the program.

3. In what ways is monitoring built into the program itself?
    The staff at the rehabilitation center had weekly conferences with Roberta to discuss her progress in the physical therapy part of the rehabilitation program. She monitored her psychological progress

through weekly meetings with a counselor. She reviewed with him the tasks she had set herself in the previous meeting. For instance, she discussed her tendency to engage in self-defeating self-talk.

4. Are there some clear indications that by implementing your plan you are moving toward your goal or subgoal? What are these indications?

Sue and Todd discovered that the number of fights and arguments per week were actually diminishing. They also discovered that the fights they did have were not as bitter as they used to be. They were fighting more fairly with each other.

5. If the goal has been totally or even partially achieved, has it lead to or is it leading to some kind of effective management of the original problem situation?

Jason's original presenting complaint was a "poor self image." This included feeling bad about his personal appearance. Since he was severely overweight, one goal was weight loss. He participated successfully in a weight loss program. When he lost a fair amount of weight, he began to feel better about himself in two ways. He felt better about his physical appearance. And he now saw himself as an agent in life rather than a victim. He was on his way to handling his "poor self-image."

Now ask these same questions of a plan of action in which you are presently engaged.

a. A summary of your goal and action plan:

_____

_____

_____

_____

_____

_____

b. Are you implementing the plan or not?

_____

c. If you are implementing it, how fully are you doing so? What are you doing? What are you failing to do?

_____

_____

_____

_____

d. What changes, if any, are needed in your plan?

_____

_____

_____

_____

e. In what ways is monitoring built into the plan itself?

_____

_____

_____

_____

f. How can you more effectively monitor your participation in the program?

_____

_____

_____

g. Are there some clear indications that by implementing this plan you are moving toward your goal or subgoal? What are these indications?

_____

_____

_____

_____

_____

h. What modifications, if any, do you have to make in your preferred scenario and goals?

_____

_____

_____

i. If your goal has been fully or even partially accomplished, has it lead to or is it leading to some kind of effective management of the original problem situation or some part of it? How can you tell?

_____

_____

_____

_____

_____

j. What kind of recycling of the problem-management process would be useful at this point?

_____

_____

_____

_____

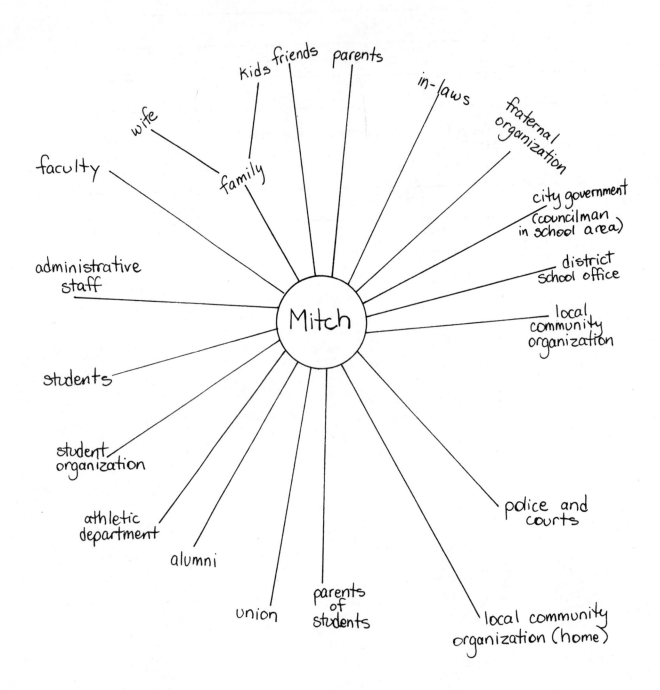